BRIGIT PEGEEN KELLY:
The Many-Mindedness of Spirit

Ricky Ray is a poet, essayist and eco-mystic who lives with his wife and the ghost of his old brown dog in the old green hills of New England. He is the author of four books of poetry, including *The Soul We Share*, winner of the Aryamati Prize, and *Quiet, Grit, Glory*. He lectures on poetry, animism and integral ecology, and he serves on the advisory board of the Program for the Evolution of Spirituality at Harvard.

Brigit Pegeen Kelly (1951-2016) was a widely admired and influential American poet, known for her striking work and her haunting, mythic imagination. She was born in Palo Alto, California, grew up in southern Indiana, died in Urbana, Illinois, and had both an artist's and a poet's training. She authored three books of poetry, including *To the Place of Trumpets*, winner of the Yale Younger Poets Award; *Song*, winner of the Lamont Poetry Prize; and *The Orchard*, a finalist for the Pulitzer Prize. She earned many of her country's most prestigious accolades, including the Discovery/*The Nation* Poetry Prize, a Whiting Award, and fellowships from the National Endowment for the Arts, the Guggenheim Foundation, and the Academy of American Poets. For decades, she served at the University of Illinois, Urbana-Champaign as a professor of creative writing, and was deeply beloved by her students.

Also by Ricky Ray

for Brigit
&
for Addie

ISBN: 978-1-916938-81-6

Cover designed by Aaron Kent

Cover image: © erna / Adobe Stock

Edited and Typeset by Aaron Kent

Broken Sleep Books Ltd
PO BOX 102
Llandysul
SA44 9BG

CONTENTS

Child. We are done for
in the most remarkable ways.
— Brigit Pegeen Kelly

The Many-Mindedness of Spirit

Ricky Ray

Broken Sleep Books

Invocation

Brigit Pegeen Kelly. The mere mention of her name invokes, for me, a shadow animal coursing around the room, the field, the world. A shadow animal at once as small as a flea's footprint, and as large as a galactic storm. The shadow animal, despite its dark nature, acts as a force of illumination. That is, it draws attention, compels contemplation, reveals things rather than hides them, even if the revelation is of a mystery, a mystery the mind can sense and heart can feel, but never grasp nor pin down like a butterfly to a board. The shadow animal is a shapeshifter, an energetic vortex, a portal, a being who can manifest itself into many beings, or none.

Tonight, in this house, as the wind howls across the top of the hill where we live on Addie's Acres, the shadow animal grows wings, wings that flutter in the corners of this *living* room, the corners where hardly anyone looks, where the spider webs and dog hair conspire to catch things, and the air stirs, as if a phantom pair of lungs had drawn breath and exhaled. Then the shadow animal enters the walls and groans, groans like the beams of dead but still-existing trees, whose ghosts shelter us against the storms, the groans of a house whose story we populate as pages, chapters, characters come and gone.

I trace the wing-flaps from the corners to the fireplace to the floors to the back porch, then the shadow animal slips out the door. I try to follow it across the garden into the family cemetery, but I find I'm following a version of myself. Someone I was before I was born. He tells me to go home, to be warm, to be grateful there is warmth amidst the cold. Grateful but careful. Shivering, my body tells me he is right, so I turn around. When I return to my chair and sip my Christmas port—a '77 Fonseca, older than I am—I can feel the shadow animal's breath entwined with mine. Entwined with my ancestor's too.

It's frightful, but Kelly's work has taught me to try to retain wonder when I'm afraid—wonder-danger: a keener sense of being alive—so I take another sip to fortify my resolve, and muse. Who is this shadow animal? *Who* isn't the question. The question is *what.* What composes and endures this continuous procession of selves, simultaneously howling and singing and breathing in my breath, this shadow animal that appears then disappears, but still resides?

The mind wants to know, but as I said, it's something dark, the feeling of a river flowing in the blood or underground.

The shadow animal invoked by Kelly's name: it might be spirit, might be will, might be a planet whose thoughts are the lives of entire species, might be the moments when an organism, like me, overhears the lungs of a galaxy breathing, then drops his jaw in awe. It might be the wonder and terror of love. It might be an ancient chorus, inviting us into the song. Having spent a good many years wandering the gifts Kelly left us, her name invokes, for me, a world that complex, that alluring, that enlightening, that strange.

I: *To the Place of Trumpets*

Brigit Pegeen Kelly was both a rarity and a mystery in late 20th-century and early 21st-century American poetry. A rarity in that she was one of our best and most-admired poets, one of eight poets in any era I wouldn't want to live without, often leading that group. Living poets, or the poets I know, generally speak of her with awe and a hushed reverence, as though the mere mention of her work were something to humble oneself before. That rarified, that rare. Kelly was also a mystery, in that she was a deeply private person, shunning interviews and literary limelight to the point that her body of work, rather than her person, is the figure we've come to know. Perhaps that's as it should be, given the depth of her achievement—its fearsome wonderment, its small but explosive force. She was a rarity, in that every poet I ever met who read her work at length was hooked, and a mystery, in that there's a dearth of scholarship on her work, a chasm of written affection, which this essay seeks in some small part to correct.

Her poems, too, are a rarity, in that they have the power to forever mark their readers, and a mystery, in that the way they mark one can be deeply uncomfortable, unsettling, a taste of something one isn't sure it was safe to imbibe, a sense that the world we see isn't the world we thought we saw. Again, as it should be, since playing it safe is how artists wallow in mediocrity, and how we ourselves tend to circle old fields of habit, blissfully and pitifully blind to the riches of perception we might experience if we stepped not just outside of our comfort zone, but deep into the woods, where the illusion of human dominance drops away, where our strangeness is made self-evident and anything might happen. By *anything*, I mean a human might crawl out of the mouth of a dog, only to do a dance that animates an ancient statue, then crawl back into the dog and continue on their strange, multi-minded journey, wandering into something far beyond human experience, far beyond words and the province of intellectual understanding.

Given the intensity of Kelly's privacy, few biographical details are readily found: born in Palo Alto, California in 1951; died in Urbana-Champaign, Illinois in October, 2016; grew up in southern Indiana; had Irish-American heritage and turned as a teenager towards a Catholic faith;[1] received early training in the

---

1. Plumepoetry.com, https://plumepoetry.com/uncovering-what-is-brave-a-remembrance-of-brigit-pegeen-kelly-by-joy-manesiotis-and-maxine-scates/, accessed December 31, 2024.

visual arts; earned her MFA at the University of Oregon; taught at various universities, settling at the University of Illinois at Urbana-Champaign, where she lived and taught alongside her husband, the poet and writer Michael David Madonick.[2] She had three children, seems to have been widely beloved by her students, cited as being extremely generous with her attention—spending, on occasion, hours discussing a feather[3]—and produced a modest output of three collections of poetry between 1987 and 2004. Except that those books were anything but modest. They were more like little bombs in the forms of books waiting for you to crack them open and light the fuse with your unsuspecting eyes. Critics and prize committees agreed, awarding her the Discovery/*The Nation* Poetry Prize (1986), the Yale Younger Poets Award (1987), the Lamont Poetry Prize (1994), a Whiting Award (1996), the Witter Byner Poetry Prize (1999), an NEA Fellowship (2005), a Guggenheim Fellowship (2006), and a Fellowship of the Academy of American poets (2008), among others. Her last book, *The Orchard*, was a finalist for the LA Times Book Award, the National Book Critics' Circle Award and the Pulitzer Prize. Had she kept writing at the standard she'd set (or better), I'm certain she would have brought home the lot. But none of that seemed to matter to her, or to matter far less than it did to most. What mattered was the work, and in poem after poem, it shows.

---

2. Enotes.com, https://www.enotes.com/topics/brigit-pegeen-kelly, accessed May 25th, 2019.
3. Michael Minucci, *Dual: Poems*, "On Brigit Pegeen Kelly," Acre Books (2023), 55.

Kelly published her first volume, *To the Place of Trumpets* (Yale University Press, 1988), at the age of thirty-seven. Selected by James Merrill for the Yale Series of Younger Poets, it weighed in at thirty-one poems and seventy pages. In it, she revealed some of the trademark tendencies that would remain central to her work: a mythic and forceful imagination; an obsession with flora and fauna, especially birds, deer, lions, cows and flowers; a fabulist tone and diction that seemed half wrought from an old porch-side storyteller, half contracted from a hermetic oracle; a talent for arresting similes and metaphors; an ear for inconspicuous rhythm that entrances with a steady and incantatory momentum; an affinity for darkness, danger and death; a sense of suffering and pleasure entwined, struggling for dominance, the struggle itself a kind of balance; an aversion to technology and the illusion of the over-empowered human; a simultaneously restrained and rhapsodic rhetoric. Most of all, she displayed an unusual and interesting mind, a mind whose habits of thinking and marveling might transform one's own.

In his introduction, Merrill said, "at the simplest level, she retains the wild, transforming eye of childhood,"[4] which is to say she hadn't dulled her capacity for wonder, nor was her wonder more full of roses than the bodies one might find beneath them. He also noted the presence of her Catholic background, the rituals and iconography which some critics say give Catholic artists a leg up

---

4. Brigit Pegeen Kelly, *To the Place of Trumpets*, Yale University Press (1988), *ix*.

on their Protestant or secular peers, but he rightly noted that she wasn't writing in service of religion. She didn't allow any hold it may have had upon her imagination to confine her art. Rather, she wandered in religion's realm and beyond, intentionally drawing from it as a source—one of many—inherent in her vision. As Merrill noted, in reference to the "shaping past" we all must contend with, "isn't the most we can do, to be free [not *of* it but] *with* it, submit it to some shaping of our own?"[5] How right he would be, for this act—participating intensely in the shaping of her vision, rather than being merely subject to its whims—Kelly would perfect to staggering effect in the years and books to come.

Kelly opens *Trumpets* with "After Your Nap," a poem written by a mother for her child, presumably for Kelly's own child, since the poem is dedicated to Maria, one of the dedicatees of Kelly's second book, but it's always hard to tell in her poems whether the first person voice or experiences relayed are personal, impersonal, or an impossible-to-discern admixture of the two. I think it's inescapably both, but she's as sly in this as she was in keeping out of the limelight. In some of her poems, she suggests that we are so bound up in one another, we are more of a mutuality than an individuality, which is to say our greater commonalities and lesser differences both tie us together and keep us just separate enough to regard one another and interact. In any case, Kelly takes the old adage of opening her collection with a strong poem seriously, and never feels more personal in her books than she does

5. Ibid, *xi*.

in her first.

Her career as a poet opens with the speaker carrying her daughter to sit on the porch—(a clue to the nature of her voice?)—where they sit before "the vast expanse of bee-studded lawn / and the blank pastel shingle of the housing opposite."[6] Already one of her enduring symbols—the bee—has a brief cameo. And then her talent for metaphor steps up:

> In an upstairs window the dim t-shirt of a man moves,
> is swallowed, returns again from shadow—a buoy
>
> indolently bobbing on a gray and mild sea.
> You roll away from me and lie on your back,
>
> the small sack of your body filling slowly with itself,
> while children careen and call
>
> and I cradle my marriage gently in my lap—
> a quiet thing, small, a thing barely breathing[7]

The synecdoche of t-shirt for the man who moves to-and-fro the window as a buoy in a sea of shadow is a clever series of moves, especially in three lines, but cleverness, at least for cleverness' sake, never feels to me like part of Kelly's repertoire. Is she, and are her poems, smart? Incredibly. But wit for the mere sake of verbal play seems anathema to her drive. No, Kelly just happens to see this way—perhaps it's her background as a painter—or to work so intently at making her vision lucid that its density is a byproduct rather than an aim. The vision of the man, after all, is a brief glimpse in a serious poem, where the child's life accrues the world—"the small sack of your body filling slowly with itself"—and where the

6. Ibid., "After Your Nap," 3.
7. Ibid.

speaker's marriage, or what's left of it, can be held, like the child, perhaps even within the child, in the speaker's lap. In these terms, the marriage and the child feel like equally frail countercurrents, wayfarers at the edge of love, one heading towards the center of the heart, the other headed out.

From there, the speaker turns her gaze back to the window, then out to the sky, "ash colored, purple to the North", and down to the fields, where grass is burning. She transfers her inner weariness to the day, to the quality of light itself, saying "the light is growing loose, the way clothes do // after having been worn for a long time." Something in her wears loose before it wears out—a position of comfort, which may also be a precursor to rags. Then birds, her great loves, arrive in their own cameo like the bees, rising and falling, and she turns back to her child, ending the poem, "I run my hand over the neat purse of your small belly / the hard knot of your pubis // and think how surely we are contained / how well our small boundaries love us."[8] While deftly composed in parts, on the whole the poem doesn't quite satisfy or feel like Kelly in full possession of her visionary powers: the last couplet is diffuse, philosophical to the point of being abstract, sweetly hopeful, wishful—the closing gesture of a young, idealistic poet, and a move Kelly would never make in her second or third books. But at the same time, I love that couplet, its motherly hope and tenderness so clear and intimate, one can practically feel the mother's hand on her child's belly, hovering in reverence, trying

8. Ibid.

to bless it against the inevitable heartbreaks and hardships. And I admire the way vision moves in the poem: from the focal point of the relationship with the child, out to the man in the window, away to the sea, back to the child, in towards the marriage, out to the sky, the fields, the light, the birds, then back again to the child and the boundaries that contain them all. Kelly would go on to become a master of discursion and digression, but already, on page one, the habits of mind leave traces, working in layers, which again hearkens back to her artist's training—a thought confirmed, perhaps, by a rare comment Kelly made on her compositional process, "you sketch, paint, paint over it. My writing method resembles the construction of art. I write a lot of drafts."[9] The poem feels to me like a rare moment of personal intimacy, the softness of entrance held protectively against the harshness of exits.

The book's second poem, "Music School," is one of Kelly's shortest, and also her least substantial in my estimation. Not a fault, necessarily, but evidence, in light of her later works, of having cultivated her powers, as much as being born into them. A little hope for us who believe in the hard work of drafts and toil. To quickly gloss the poem, Kelly considers birds in a bush as instruments of some song in which they are held, but which they cannot get right. She pounds on the wall but they won't stop. The lines are prosy, presumptuous, slight: "they practice so hard and never get it right," and "they think that the whole world is

9. Enotes.com, https://www.enotes.com/topics/brigit-pegeen-kelly, accessed May 25th, 2019.

chortling." I'm hard on this poem not because it's a bad poem—it's competent and contains wonder—but to work toward an estimation that might approach Kelly's own.

Like many artists, she seems to have been embarrassed by her first book, or at least to hold it in a less than favorable light than her subsequent accomplishments. Her student Corey Miller reports that Kelly "told me Yale had protested multiple times because she refused to allow them the right to reprint her first book",[10] and to this day I believe it remains out of print. Irish poet Eavan Boland similarly remarked that Kelly "spoke lightly—almost off-handedly—of wanting to suppress her first book" since she "was not satisfied with the work in it."[11] In fairness, her dissatisfaction is justified in light of the work to come, and in the sense that several of the poems carry on beyond their proper ending, or strive for endings they haven't fully earned, but her sense of the book lacking in its entirety is hers alone, for it holds many fine poems, visions and revelations in their own right. As a critic, I choose to see it as a book of great promise with moments of the incredible power she would continuously yield later on, and as a poet, I'm grateful for the opportunity to trace the arc of her development. Only tertiarily do I regard it as a book containing a young poet's usual oversights and missteps. I'm calling Kelly young at thirty-seven, which some might not agree with, but consider that Frost published his first at

---

10. Medium.com, https://medium.com/@coreymiller/remember-ing-brigit-pegeen-kelly-569124086ce6, accessed May 25th, 2019.
11. Web.archive.org, https://web.archive.org/web/20180204214252/http://poems.com/special_features/prose/essay_boland_kelly.php, accessed May 25th, 2019.

thirty-eight, Moore at thirty-four, and Stevens at forty-four, and in that fine company, she's right on the mark.

I'll spend less time with her first book than her mature standouts, but a few of her early habits and exceptional poems deserve their place alongside the siblings they would pave the way for. At heart, I think Kelly's a visionary storyteller who happens to be a poet, and this gets truer and truer over the course of her career. She's also an ornate lyricist who happens to think in stories. This convergence of approaches to language and event— approaches from the side of music and the side of lore—accounts, I think, for much of Kelly's appeal: as stories ourselves, we feel at home in narration, but we want the language of those stories to be so remarkably rich and enthralling, it elevates us out of our usual pitch. And elevate she does.

In the long, serial poem "Sundays," a man's smile becomes not only a positive facial expression, but a figurative enlargement of welcome:

> [...] And when he smiles
> his head comes forward
> and his teeth come forward
> as if he brought his fence out farther
> to make the yard larger
> to let more people in.[12]

The wonderment it takes to make this imaginative leap is precisely one of the things I turn to poetry for, Kelly in particular: that my own wonderment might be revived, increased and restored. Later in the poem, she takes a more lyrical turn, revealing how her

12. Brigit Pegeen Kelly, *To the Place of Trumpets*, "Sundays", Yale University Press (1988), 9.

hyper-focus can both transform the world at hand, and guide the eye to the minute details that generally pass us by—the kind of attention that sears a moment into memory:

> And the lost calf—little
> lily-breathed, tufted-bird-feather
> furred—is now in the field,
> with the bigger cows nosing him
> and the Rose of Sharon dropping
> pink bathwater
> all down his back.[13]

Several of her characteristic traits are on display here: the animal subject, something of the bird inhering in the mammal, the hand that flora play in the life of fauna—the Rose of Sharon, a member of the Hibiscus family, is a key totem that returns often throughout her books—and the deceptively simple, straightforward diction that somehow seems wrung from a higher register. This last trait is a key aspect of Kelly's magic: she traffics in the elemental—animals, plants, atmosphere, attention—and in the simple—monosyllables, everyday vernacular—and yet the way she blends them together and doses them with a touch of the ineffable, one can hardly help but be captivated by her verbal skill. As if her words were presences meant not merely to communicate images but to summon worlds for the reader to inhabit, body and soul.

Her word choice reminds me of Hemingway's retort to Faulkner, who accused Hemingway of not having the courage to use words that might send a reader to the dictionary. Old Hem's reply was a splendid defense of the common style: "Poor Faulkner.

---

13. Ibid., 12

Does he really think big emotions come from big words? He thinks I don't know the ten-dollar words. I know them all right. But there are older and simpler and better words, and those are the ones I use."[14] This invocation, of long-ripening (and long-festering) pools of vocabulary within language, and within the spirit of the species, says volumes about Kelly's word choice, and her choice of subject matter, equally long-ripening and long-festering within creaturely consciousness. Most of her poems could have happened five-hundred years ago as easily as today.

Generally, Kelly dwells in darkness. Feels at home there. And to enter a Kelly poem is to enter a realm where danger tugs the air, and something has gone wrong, or probably will. But she's capable of sudden joyous leaps, as well. In "Queen Elizabeth and the Blind Girl or Music for the Dead Children," she follows a boy dragging a stick along an iron fence, "His limbs leap like warm marigolds. The fence // rails are people. They clap. They clap. *O fine* / they say *O fine fine fine* and the whole sky wings down."[15] Notice, again, the inventive floral simile, the rails suddenly springing to life as the stick clatters along, and the smart use of wing as a verb to catch the inner lightening in which the sky comes down and seems embodied within a moment of exuberance. Such untempered highs are rare in Kelly's work, and perhaps, in an age of false emphasis and melodrama, they retain their height by being

14. A.E. Hotchner, *Papa Hemingway: A Personal Memoir*, Da Capo Press (2005), 69-70.
15. Brigit Pegeen Kelly, *To the Place of Trumpets*, "Queen Elizabeth and the Blind Girl or Music for the Dead Children," Yale University Press (1988), 17.

few and far between.

A more typical character is the woman in "Young Wife's Lament" who says "Some of us / have mule minds," "some of us are not given / even a wheel of the tinker's cart / upon which to pray."[16] How true that providence isn't equally or consistently apportioned, and yet, what is given, however little, is enough upon which to pray, even if it's only one's own squalid breath. Or consider the dog in "Harmony Stoneworks, Late Winter": "This is where / the spaniel comes, where alleys of stubble fill / with darkness and wash him toward me—one-eyed spaniel, / filthy, wearing his patched body like a madman's coat,"[17] the prototype of an interspecies creature who will appear in a late, staggering poem, "The Dance."

To the Place of Trumpets also contains, for me, the most troubling poem in her oeuvre, a strong statement given the dark and sometimes macabre nature of her work. Simply titled "Dog," this one hits me squarely in moral revulsion territory, because it easily could have happened, and not just within a vision. The dog, "a gentle mongrel," was hit by a truck. It died "slowly on a heap of rags... / its back legs crushed, soiling itself / as it tried to rise, and howling howling."[18] Were that all, I'd be sad but moved. But Kelly habitually pushes past where most poets would come to rest, pushes past the borders of where they'd dare not go. She pushes herself, and us, into "the smell of urine and old cement", and

16. Ibid., "Young Wife's Lament," 30-31.
17. Ibid., "Harmony Stoneworks, Late Winter," 23.
18. Ibid., "Dog," 28.

pushes further, into the speaker's fear:

> And because the smells
> frightened you and the way the dog threw back
> his head and would not listen, and how
> his eyes, yellowed with pain, would not see,
> and how in his head as he cried he went on
> walking, walking, wherever it was he walked,
> you kicked him to stop the noise,
> kicked and kicked, as if you were kicking
> the loud wheel of the truck that struck him,
> as if you were that wheel itself [19]

Honestly, the poem makes me want to kick the speaker until she yelps. And keep on kicking until she spits blood. And then, to concoct a long night of torture. Yet, when that furious rage begins to subside, I admit that the response arises, in part, because I can imagine myself in her position, driven to the same edge, likely to end the dog's misery in a quicker, more brutal fashion, or to drug him into oblivion, but who knows?

If similar deliriums that gripped the speaker gripped me, and if, under the spell of that derangement, I found myself in the same circumstances, how would my organism respond? Which compulsions which would I be bent by fate to obey; which could I allay? I don't know, but I know how my being, in this moment, feels. There are plenty of cruelnesses explored in Kelly's work, and that work is welcome to wander and influence nearly the whole of my heart, but I'd give her even more room had she chosen not to publish this. That's my limitation, not hers, and I'm grateful to her for forcing me to confront one of my own limits. As Kelly's student

---

19. Ibid., 28-29.

Darcie Dennigan noted, "It is my love for Brigit that gives me the company, I won't say courage, but company to look at these things I cannot look at alone."[20] That rings true for me, too—it's because I love Kelly's work that I trust her enough to keep reading. And I'm glad to be aware of that dark path, where it might lead, but I do not wish to walk its plank or answer its call. If I did, I can see what might happen in the sense of what I would do to the dog's abuser. That Kelly could—and did—go there, I nod towards in grudging respect. And when I close the book and turn it over, I'm met with a smile and a saving grace: a picture of Kelly and her dog, her face turned towards him with a look of affection, her hands buried in his fur with love. I could, and did, imagine the death of my soul dog, Addie, many times while she was alive, but I could not have imagined her abuse. That would have wrecked me. I imagine it wrecked Kelly, too, but she had the sheer force of will to look misery in the face, and to carry us with her.

Another of Kelly's gifts is the gift of transformation. The ability to turn an ordinary moment or sensation into something far more complicated and alive, possessed of its own being and intentions. It's also the ability to hold the many layers that comprise a feeling in mind, and to carry us from one window to another, that we might witness the layers shifting. Take a moment in church, for example. In "Imagining Their Own Hymns," Kelly considers the angels in the stained glass windows, who, rather

20. Kenyonreview.org, https://kenyonreview.org/kr-online-is-sue/2020-septoct/selections/darcie-dennigan-656342/, accessed December 29, 2024.

than beatific agents of beneficence, "have mean lit faces", "do not love the light" and grow so "sick of Jesus, / who never stops dying", they eventually decide to make a break for it: "as in a wedding march, / their pockets full of money from the boxes / for the sick poor, they will walk down the aisle," away from the cross, "imagining their own hymns".[21] The scene seems wrought from the mind of mischievous child, and yet, there's something teenage at play in the act of rebellion, and something even more mature in the fullness of the life-changing decision to abandon both duty and values. To have no hymns of one's own, to see a fuller path and make a hymn in defiance—can we blame them for breaking rank?

Three more poems, before we bid *Trumpets* goodbye. "The House on Main Street" is a prime example of the way Kelly holds bitterness and sweetness on the same tongue, the way she finds a path to gratitude in the destitution of fallen feathers: "as if by gripping them / in our palms, or / stuffing them in our coats, we can be / connected with flight, not with the stone angels / shadowing the frozen / ground, but with a body / that has truly flown, with a mind / that makes the sky / its home."[22] There's a longing for the avian in Kelly, favoring birds over even angels, a longing to be able to shift from the sinking stones of heartache to the buoyant feather-lifts of flight. But she knows she can't stay there long. The poem returns to Earth and ends in a cemetery,

21. Ibid., "Imagining Their Own Hymns," 40-41.
22. Ibid., "The House on Main Street," 53.

another of her recurring haunts, in this case a pet cemetery, where the animals:

> were never under their fancy markers at all
> but had been thrown behind the lake
> into huge pits that poisoned all the wells
> along Willow Run with their decay.
> It grows warm then cold. Along the roads
> possums fall beneath our tires. Some years
> are years for dying, as they are for fire.[23]

Every time, the strokes of genius in those seven lines, especially the last one, gives me chills: the way that humanity's disrespectful treatment of beloved companion species—throwing their bodies in huge pits—ultimately spoils the waters that nourish or poison us all. The way misdeeds come back to bite us. The way nature operates by birth and beauty, yes, but also by death and karma. The years warm, the years cold, the years when both useful roads and beautiful possums fall beneath our tires, and the years when the tires of dying and fires come spinning straight towards us. Sometimes I think that if one eye saw elation, and one eye saw anguish, I might get a sense of what it was like to live in Kelly's head.

The poem I find myself turning to most often in *Trumpets* is one of the briefest and sparest Kelly wrote, "The White Deer." She excelled at long, intricate narratives, but this one says exactly what it needs to say in a handful of overlapping images that pummel me and leave me with the relief—if can be called relief—of one final *whew* of exhalation:

---

23. Ibid., 54.

The sister was mad
and so must be forgiven,
mad as the deer
trapped in the cow field,
over and again
it threw itself at the fences,
leaping in that leaping
that is not running but flight,
bloodying its mouth,
bloodying its chest,
four blood spots
like hand prints on its neck,
frenzied by those
who helpless would yet help it,
the man and his wife
flapping like large birds
veering this way and that
to head it to the gate,
while the hawk and its thirst
flew low over the cornfield,
flew low toward the promise
of the deer hanging high,
high on the fence
with its head dropped down,
like the hand of a girl
who has given it all up,
who has looked to the sky
and to those who would help her
and has laid her soft head
on the ground.[24]

One could spend a dozen pages peeling back the layers. It reminds
me that a self, a person, an organism, is not an independence but
an interdependence, a nexus of beings and belongings within
which each of us is both a network and a node, a process and a
being, as much Earth as we are human, as much girl as we are deer,
as much life as we are organism, longing to help a dying animal
with our hands, our hands compelled by the same power that

---

24. Ibid., "The White Deer," 35.

leaves smudges of blood on the deer's neck, the blood in the deer belonging as much to the hunger in the hawk's belly as to the deer's will to live, the urge to live inevitably exhausting and retiring one body to take up residence in countless others, residing and retiring until the urge to be retires the urge to live and puts the body of life itself to rest. All of this, and I haven't even asked: why was the sister mad? Did her madness, perhaps, scare the deer across the field and onto the fence? This cacophony of vectors and voices coalesced into a scene so masterfully paced and framed—Kelly's best traits at that age, and in any age, seem to me on full display.

The book's title poem, "The Place of Trumpets," is a departure from the others in its overt anaphora, its clipped phrases and its nearness to psalm. It seems to me a vision of heaven. I offer a generous quoting to convey its gist and power: "To the place of trumpets /.../ ...where peace sits, // We are going." "Where all who wake, wake undone, /.../ Back to where self is song, // Where the unmade hands are wheels, /.../ And the heart the child that kneels // and never tires". "Where West // Marries East, and trust turns / To betrayal as its friend, / Where days and moon and sins are one / Blessed wind passing over / The passing plains, over / The sea, the comforter // Full of salt so sweet it fills / The hollow tongue until / It splits as time will // Split and spill its tattered toys". "Where the wound loves the arrow / Where ankle and adder know // Accord, where the lion's lamb / Leads him to the grasses down, / Leads him with her little song".[25] The poem—nay, song—cascades

25. Ibid., "The Place of Trumpets," 64-65.

with incantatory power and sings its being better than I could ever explain its meaning. Here the half of Kelly born of the oracle presides—the power of vision born into song, which, for the next seven years, would weigh heavy on her mind.

II: *Song*

Brigit Pegeen Kelly's second collection saw her move to a well-regarded American indie press, and garnered the Academy of American Poets Lamont Poetry Prize, which gave the volume significant exposure. While working on the collection, individual poems found their way into two volumes of *Best American Poetry* (1993 and 1994) and earned her a Pushcart Prize (1995). The collection picks up where "The Place of Trumpets" left off, in *Song* (BOA Editions, 1995).[26] Like her first book, *Song* opens with power in "Song," which frankly is a gargantuan understatement. It opens with a knockout of a poem, and I mean a knocked-it-the-fuck-out-of-the-ballpark

26. Note: *Song* and Kelly's subsequent book, *The Orchard*, were re-published in a single volume in 2008 by Carcanet Press in the UK. The Carcanet volume was my reference source for this book, hence the forthcoming citations.

and knocked-a-little-dust-off-the-moon and is-still-out-there-knocking-through-the-stars kind of knockout. By many accounts, it's the best poem she ever wrote, one for the canon, and I'd doubt the memory of anyone who ever read it and claimed they couldn't remember. It's known informally as her "goat head" poem, a sixty-four-line affair that runs through the reader like a freight train whose only mercy is obliteration. This probably sounds like hyperbole, and sure, mayhaps, but some poems earn the boast. Consider briefly Danniel Schoonebeek's account of hearing Kelly recite the work in 2008, the account shared shortly after Kelly's death in 2016:

> "She opened with "Song," and to this day it was the greatest, not one of the greatest, the greatest reading of a poem I've ever witnessed in my life. All around the auditorium people were gasping and holding their hands over their mouths like some terrible onus had just been placed upon their heads. A lot of people near me were crying like confused kids in horror movies. I remember my friend Christina leaning over to me and saying she felt like she'd just gotten baptized."[27]

This sounds less like the account of a poem recitation than one of a Pentecostal tent revival. When poets and publishers say to open with your best, this is the kind of effect they're after. How could you not read the rest after being possessed and forever altered by the first piece in the book?

Sadly, the poem's too long to reproduce here, but it deserves to be read in full. If you haven't, put this book down and do. Here's a link, so you don't even have to search:

27. Facebook.com, https://www.facebook.com/danniel.schoonebeek/posts/10100463372594864, accessed May 26th, 2019.

https://poets.org/poem/song.

The poem opens:

> Listen: there was a goat's head hanging by ropes in a tree.
> All night it hung there and sang. And those who heard it
> Felt a hurt in their hearts and thought they were hearing
> The song of a night bird. They sat up in their beds, and then
> They lay back down again. In the night wind, the goat's head
> Swayed back and forth, and from far off it shone faintly
> The way the moonlight shone on the train track miles away
> Beside which the goat's headless body lay. Some boys
> Had hacked its head off. It was harder work than they had imagined.[28]

At once we're in the realm of the terrible and strange. Who would hang a goat's head in a tree, and why? And how on Earth could it hang there all night and sing? This is Kelly's task, to show us the confluence of forces by which such heinous and impossible occurrences come to pass, and transgress against our expectations, perhaps even against our imaginations. She willingly throws herself into the vision, mind and soul, knowing, I think, that we have much to learn from it, though I can only guess that composing such a fright-scape was anything but pleasant. The perpetrators were, of course, boys, humoring the impulse to violence they couldn't understand, committing the kind of act that scars the soul for life, whether to teach it a lesson and better it, or to ruin it by giving it a taste.

The "song" the goat-head sings is more than just its cry. It is of the "night bird" and of the hurt that its listeners carry in their hearts. It is of the light of which both head and body, parts

---

28. Brigit Pegeen Kelly, *Song and The Orchard*, "Song," Carcanet Press, Ltd. (2008), 13.

and wholes, are made. It is of magnetism, for when head and body
were separated:

> They missed each other. The missing grew large between them,
> Until it pulled the heart right out of the body, until
> The drawn heart flew toward the head, flew as a bird flies
> Back to its cage and the familiar perch from which it trills.[29]

That the heart roosts in the head, that it may even rule the head, we
know, though we may, in what we call our cooler moments, believe
otherwise. But passion animates the blood. When the light came
up, the singing stopped, and many lyric poets would end there,
but that's only the beginning of Kelly's story, which properly has a
beginning, a middle and an end. The goat belonged to a girl, who
named it "Broken Thorn Sweet Blackberry," a girl who brushed
him and fed him and sang to him, who dreamed him bigger and so
bigger he became. When she woke to the empty yard, she knew—
her heart knew—that harm had befallen him. Still, she sought
him out, calling and calling while "the stones goug[ed] the soft
undersides / Of her bare feet",[30] a brilliant detail on Kelly's part to
cite even the ground's complicity in the girl's woe. The townsfolk
hurried to hide the body and raise money for another goat, well-
intentioned but misguided acts.

Then, we enter the third movement of the poem, the
state of the boys' souls. They said it was a joke, as if they could kid
themselves, as if they could ever escape that night. As if they could
somehow evade the things their hands did, the hands heavy with

29. Ibid.
30, Ibid., 14.

guilt and harm at ends of their own arms. "What they didn't know, / Was that the goat's head would go on singing, just for them, / Long after the ropes were down," and "they would

> Wake in the night thinking they heard the wind in the trees
> Or a night bird, but their hearts beating harder. There
> Would be a whistle, a hum, a high murmur, and, at last, a song,
> The low song a lost boy sings remembering his mother's call.
> Not a cruel song, no, no, not cruel at all. This song
> Is sweet. It is sweet. The heart dies of this sweetness.[31]

As a reader, I'm gutted. As a poet, I'm in awe: who among us would have the turn of mind to let the goat's song offer the boys a path of return to motherly good? A path of redemption, where the boys might learn to suppress the demons in their hands, locking them behind skeletal bars. Or not. Some respond to being haunted by guilt with fear, some with remediation, some with self-destruction, some with violence. Who among us would call the haunting sweet? A sweetness that, as sugar does, rots the heart until it dies.

 I like to believe there's another side to this sweetness. A sweetness the girl knows. A sweetness the head knows of the heart. The sweetness of the song that sings girl to goat, heart to head, life to body, boys to mothers, bodies to ground—a sweetness that kills us all the same, but a killing of relationships lived to the end of their wick, not murder, a dying of love for this life we lived and those we shared it with, not a dying of dread for the misdeeds we did when we were dumb and could. Both kinds of sweetness—dark and light—are available to us, and in all likelihood, most lives bear

---

31. Ibid.

an ever-fluctuating mixture of the two. But even in mixture, there's a dominate note. At death, which note do we end on? Which note prevails? Kelly rightly does not say, and leaves it for us to find out.

It's hard to know how to proceed. "Song" is a blazing narrative introduction to what paradoxically was Kelly's most lyrical book. Many consider it her best. For my part, it depends on the day. When I want song, when I want a touch of linguistic madness, when I want to chew on a sliver of the poet's tongue, it's to *Song* I turn. When I want the shivering inner vision of the oracle, when I want a worm in my ear, when I want near flawless narrative so filled with dark myth and despair it could give Cormac McCarthy a run for his money, I turn to *The Orchard*, which, poem for poem, has for me a slight edge. But, as I say, it depends on the day's toll and the kind of liquor best suited to appease it. That choice isn't what makes it hard to move forward. The difficulty lies in the overwhelming strength of so many poems in both books. And the desire to commend them all. Put another way, I wore out a highlighter freshly decapped at the beginning of *Trumpets* while two-thirds of the way through *Song*. And I wore out another by the end of *The Orchard*. Just as Kelly's dense poems often leave more of the page filled than blank, much of my yellow overwhelms her ink.

So let us allot the essay a handful of poems per book and see where we land. But before we dive in, a little aside. Critics have pointed out that Kelly likely plays on the fact that the etymology of the word tragedy traces to the Greek for "goat song," because the "goat was either the prize in a competition of choral dancing," or "that around which a chorus danced prior to the animal's ritual sacrifice."[32] In reality, Kelly said that she had no knowledge of the etymological relation at the time of writing,[33] but if she somehow intuited it subconsciously, I tend to think her subconscious would allude to the latter interpretation. And there are, indeed, many religious, philosophical and historical allusions scattered throughout her work, but her books don't have the feel of the allusive to me. She neither parades her knowledge in front of the reader, nor requires the reader's familiarity with cultural artifacts in order to catch many of her voluminous intimations and meanings. Does familiarity breed subtle delights? Sure, but I'd even go so far as to say I'm not convinced that unfamiliarity impoverishes the reader while inhabiting Kelly's work, since the uninitiated may enjoy a freedom of association—a wider field of possibilities—that catching the reference might narrow in the specificity of its beam.

Birds. *To the Place of Trumpets* had birds winging through many of its poems, but *Song* is undoubtedly Kelly's birdiest book, with our feathered overseers populating nearly every poem with such presence, one could wonder if the song at the heart of the book is more theirs than ours. A song we inherit from them, along with an invitation to join in the Earthly chorus. The heart in "Song," for instance, flew to the head "as the bird flies" and

32. Wikipedia.org, https://en.wikipedia.org/wiki/Tragedy, accessed May 26th, 2019.
33. Kenyonreview.org, https://kenyonreview.org/kr-online-is-sue/2020-septoct/selections/darcie-dennigan-656342/, accessed December 29, 2024.

perched in the skull "from which it trill[ed]".[34] Then there's "Of Royal Issue," the book's second poem, which opens: "The sun only a small bird flitting, a wren / in the stripped forsythia, of little / note."[35] This *little note* might seem a diminishment of both sun and wren, but first impressions in Kelly rarely last. A boy watches the bird and loses interest. A bush blooms—Rose of Sharon?—and the wren speaks for it, its words "of royal issue" and now "worthy of note." The worth having always been there, our awareness of it, not so much. Then the poem takes a turn towards rhapsody—a swift ascent capped by a heart-rending image that makes the air, for me, begin to glow above the page:

> [...] O little bird,
>   how small you are, small enough to fit in a palm,
> no contender, a featherweight. Perhaps
>   we can pay the boy to trick you out of the bush,
> and trap you, and bring you in to this spot
>   by the window where your little song may
> amount to more than a tablespoon's worth of salt.
>   The glass will quicken your call, multiply it,
> multiply your nervous figure and your habit
>   of play, until you are not one bird but a hundred,
> not one tongue but a thousand, sweet prophesy
>   of the wind lighting the white strips
> of the bed sheets the boy will tear and tie
>   to the black branches of all the garden's trees,
> for no reason, because his hands
>   will not stop, *bird in the mind, bird in the bush*,
> the bird of the blood brightening
>   as it calls and calls for its mate.[36]

Again, as in "The White Deer," there's a touch—or more than a touch—of madness, of the boy's impulses overruling reason. Again,

34. Brigit Pegeen Kelly, *Song and The Orchard*, "Song," Carcanet Press, Ltd. (2008), 13.
35. Ibid., "Of Royal Issue," 15.
36. Ibid., 15-16.

there's a conflation of the avian and human such that the calls of the blood seem more of their nature than ours, or at least inherited from them, who live far more of their lives in song. Whose time on this Earth is three-hundred and thirty-three times the length of ours. Who still outnumber us six to one and have much more practice weathering extinction's storms. One could spend pages cataloguing their lines in the book, let alone their import, but for our purposes, let us sit with their names—sparrow, wren, finch, perch, redbird, jay, dove, turkey, crow, robin, swan—and let us savor the redbird "bursting his small buttons against the glass",[37] and "the junketing sparrows, briefly / Briefly, their flurries like small wine spills",[38] and even death as "a bird shadow / On the sill."[39]

And let us know that they, and the others—the bats, cicadas and wingedness penetrating the ecology of things—will inescapably lighten and darken the pages ahead. David Baker, in his review of the book for *Poetry*, noted the prevalence of our feather folk casting shadows, warnings and signs, saying, "they seem to indicate types of providential suggestion, like accompaniments or spiritual equivalents. They are a language to be interpreted, a celestial music to be learned."[40] I'd take it a step further and say theirs is a language of communion and survival, a language we should hope to become well versed in, the language of living beings communicating in sync with the life that sings them, a life they inhabit and share, not merely

37. Ibid., "A Live Dog Being Better Than a Dead Lion," 19.
38. Ibid., "Of Ancient Origins and War," 26.
39. Ibid., "Past the Stations," 57.
40. David Baker, "On Restraint: *Song* by Brigit Pegeen Kelly," *Poetry*, Vol. 168, No. 1 (April 1996), 41.

a life they possess or want. And Kelly's recurring invocation of avian persistence and importance seems to me a "providential suggestion" that we should pay them heed—they, who have endured the depths of harm and flown through the heights of life's soul far further than we could ever know.

One of the traits I love best about Kelly's work is the hierarchical demotion of humans, who, in most poets' work, rule the day and form the loci around which all else revolves. In Kelly's work, on the other hand, humans and their concerns are present, but as threads in a weave rather than the purpose of the carpet. This isn't really a demotion but an appropriate placement of us as vulnerable members of the life community, and of geo- and ecological processes that make a mockery of the inflated sense of importance of our short-lived species. As the poet Eleanor Wilner—another of my foundational influences—once said, "I love poets who bring us to our proper size."[41]

So when Kelly chooses to focus intently on a person or human scene, it's usually worth sitting up and taking notice. In "The Music Lesson," there's a little talk of the weather, then a boy enduring a piano lesson. How boring, for him and for us, lest the poet make good on the promise to transmute the lead to gold. Does she ever. At first, the boy's hands are "stiff with recalcitrant / Notes, but still the ghost hammers / Leap."[42] Then providence comes in: "lightning

41. Eleanor Wilner, "Introduction," *Ploughshares*, Vol. 35, No. 1 (Spring 2009), 7.
42. Brigit Pegeen Kelly, *Song* and *The Orchard*, "The Music Lesson," Carcanet Press, Ltd. (2008), 25.

/ Partitions the dusk—illuminating / Our brief lease—and with //
a cocksure infusion of heat / Luck lays hands on / The boy's hands
and prefigures / The pleasure that will one day / Possess this picture
for good." A little help from above goes a long way in "illuminating
our brief lease", a reminder that even our hands have movements
we don't make. Movements we are blessed (and cursed) to behold.
Movements biological, ecological, universal.

Then, Kelly complicates the picture, saying "*this* is the stone
the builders / Rejected. Pleasure. *Pleasure.*" Who are these builders
and why are they rejecting pleasure? An endlessly answerable
question, but it seems to me the builders are the forces of making—
of the world, of ability—and that they reject pleasure as an element
of sound construction—a stone—because the pleasure will be had as
an aftereffect of the making, of the made, once the work has earned
it. Of course, it may also be that the piano teacher's a strict knuckle-
rapper who favors proficiency over enjoyment. In which case, fuck
her. But to persist, to persevere despite the challenges of learning
and dispiriting boredom, is to honor the providence, to develop the
skill, and to pursue pleasure as:

> The liquid tool, the golden
> Fossil that will come to fuel
>
> In lavish and unspeakable ways
> All the dry passages
> The boy does not now comprehend
>
> Or care for. And then his
> Stricken hands will blossom
> Fat with brag. And play.[43]

43. Ibid.

Was Kelly not a recipient of her own providential stroke of luck when she thought to cast the boy's hands as growing flora that will "blossom / Fat with brag. And play."? It makes me want to turn the clock back twenty-five years, hunt down or replace the flute some miscreant stole from me, and never let it go. And that final line so etched itself into my being it opened a poem of my own. It occurs to me now that each poem does this: offer a chance to continue the music, to pick up the note and carry it forward, to leave it for others to pick up and carry, the music preceding and outlasting us, who appear briefly in its score.

Aside from birds and humans, one of Kelly's most recurring creatures is the deer, often one that comes to harm, and in the end, I think the deer is the strongest presence in her work. Recall that in "The White Deer," we saw a doe hang herself on the fence. Elsewhere, someone guns a truck and "the doe [is] thrown wide",[44] or alternately, several deer are shot and strapped "upside down to the tailgates / ...so that the deer's necks arch back as ours do / In sex",[45] or, in "All Wild Animals Were Once Called Deer," they make a ghostly sound, driven:

> Through the woods at night, white lightning through the trees,
> Through the coldest moments, when it feels as if the earth
> Will never again grow warm, lover running toward lover,
> The branches tearing back, the mouth and eyes wide,
> The heart flying into the arms of the one that will kill her.[46]

Whether driven by fear of a predator or by the pull of a lover, their

---

44. Ibid., "All Animals Were Once Called Deer," 70.
45. Ibid., "The Witnesses," 62.
46. Ibid., "All Animals Were Once Called Deer," 74.

fate seems inescapably tragic. But there's more to these proceedings than the brutal mowing down of Bambi. In Kelly's work, animals often pull double or triple duty, living their lives, and acting as totems, as portals, as points of entry for Kelly's meditations to find their genesis, the shapes of the portals shaping her journeys. Then in long, slow, methodical inquiries, her meditations reveal their secrets. Fifty lines into the poem above, Kelly discovers through the doe, who "looked alive", that "death seems to be the living thing, the thing / That looks out through the eyes."[47] In other words, death has its own movement and energy, its own "life," and could even be said to be the very continuity between lives while they switch forms, and further, that great womb from which life emerges and into which it subsides. In this sense, death is the thing that lives, each life a temporary face it wears. Each heart a portal into life-transcending feeling. In "Botticelli's St. Sebastian," Kelly claims to "*have seen* the heart / Move like a doe through the woods, move / Like a stunned doe," the trees closing behind her "the way water closes over a dropped stone, / Or a torn limb, or a lasting wound".[48] These mounting possibilities deepen the lesson at hand: the heart "flies like a bird", and it moves like a stunned deer, or an injured limb, or a wound so deep and lasting it's assuaged only by the cleansing waters of time.

Kelly's best deer poem in the book, and one of her most famous, is "Dead Doe," an atypical poem in which her narrative

47. Ibid., 72.
48. Ibid., "Botticelli's St. Sebastian," 69.

shatters and her syntax proceeds in an unsteady, surge-and-retreat motion across the page, asserting positions and immediately cancelling them out, the assertions and cancellations advancing in ghostly form. The poem opens with a mother and child observing a dead doe at a bus stop—"her belly white as a cut pear"[49]—seeing things, then unseeing them to get them right:

> The doe lay dead on her back in a field of asters: no.
>
> The doe lay dead on her back beside the school bus stop: yes.[50]

The willingness to revise experience in service of accuracy is important, the importance of being honest with ourselves about our lives, and the importance of being open to what might be happening against our initial impressions or expectations. The mother and child keep the doe's "dead run in sight, that we might see if she chose / to go skyward; / that we might run, too, turn tail / if she came near and troubled our fear with presence", a frightening thought, for:

> We can take the gilt-edged strolling of the clouds: yes.
> But the risen from the dead: no![51]

Maybe that's not true, maybe we could take it, but as a mother standing beside her child, one can hardly blame her for not wanting to chance it. And yet, she pushes further, opens to a deeper possibility, that there's more mothering going on than meets the eye, that death, "the living thing" looking through the doe's eyes, may be mothering her as well, for:

49. Ibid., "Dead Doe," 35.
50. Ibid.
51. Ibid.

> the dead can mother nothing...nothing
> but our sight[52]

Isn't one of a mother's most precious and fundamental duties to teach her children how to see? This is quite enough for a powerful poem, but Kelly refuses to relent. Her own vision's still in training. From a distance, the doe's legs, "up and frozen", look like "two swans" coupling or "stabbing the ground for some prize / worth nothing, but fought over, so worth *that*"[53]—the continual re-visioning is tantamount to enlightenment, and still, the best is yet to come:

> And this is the soul: like it or not. Yes: the soul comes down: yes: comes into the deer: yes: who dies: yes: and in her death twins herself into swans: fools us with mist and accident into believing her newfound finery
>
> and we are not afraid
> though we should be
>
> and we are not afraid as we watch her soul fly on: paired
>
> as the soul always is: with itself:
>   with others.
>   Two swans....
>
> Child. We are done for
> in the most remarkable ways.[54]

David Baker says "the astonishing double transformation—the doe into swans, and the swans into the soul—is Kelly at her finest".[55] At first, I'm inclined to agree, but then I find my own vision needs refinement. To move on from that remarkable image and admit what a mother loathes to admit, that we are slayed both by what we

---

52. Ibid.
53. Ibid., 36-37
54. Ibid., 37.
55. David Baker, "On Restraint: *Song* by Brigit Pegeen Kelly," *Poetry*, Vol. 168, No. 1 (April 1996), 44.

see (the deer) and what we are (the soul), that the wondrous can be a danger we should be afraid of, and to find the binding of danger and wonder teachable—that we should look and feel past fear, past danger, past our being "done for" into the remarkable splendor of all the ways that do us in—*that* seems to me Kelly's utmost genius in this poem. And perhaps further: that we can be done in—done-in by heart or done-in by life—and still have more to do.

I would like now to highlight a few philosophical positions and social commentaries strewn throughout *Song*. While Kelly's meanings are as layered as phyllo dough or the soil of a climax ecosystem, and while her narratives usually have a moral layer ripe for inference, she doesn't often break the story to comment on the human condition *per se*. When she does, the gesture feels personal, passionate, as if the stance or statement literally could not be withheld. Several such moments appear in "Pipistrelles," a common bat species that Kelly uses to wrestle with the bridge between the human and avian. Comparing us to bats, she says:

> [...] it is different with us. Fear in us
> Is central. Of the bone. It is our inheritance.
> Our error. What flies back at us
>
> From the rocks and trees, from the emptiness
> We cannot resist casting into,
> Is colored by the distortions of our hearts,
>
> And what we hear almost always blinds us.
> We stumble against phantoms, throw
> Ourselves from imaginary cliffs, and at dusk, like children we
>
> Run the long shadows down. Because the heart, friend,
> *Is* a shadow, a domed dark

Hung with remembered doings.[56]

Here is the voice of the familiar, the friend, breaking through the poem's invisible barrier to address the reader directly and confess some of her own hard-won insight. Kelly's vision is, as we might expect by now, rather bleak, but, to me at least, it seems to get much right: we *are* afraid—of death, of the dark, of the unknown, of each other—and it does fly back at us, if for no other reason than we imbue projections with our fear, and fear with our projections, and so receive our boomerang impressions that strike with scary discolorations. Many of the fears are founded. In "Guest Place," Kelly speaks of our "unthinking cruelty. Our own genius for harm," a genius that seems to grow more exacting and capable of devastation by the day. But we also enlarge our fears and let them, through our own anxieties and worries, terrorize us into silence, inaction and dread. We rehearse our doom and "throw / ourselves from imaginary cliffs". This state of affairs is well known, but Kelly goes one step further and calls the heart itself a shadow, a "domed dark / hung with remembered doings," as if it were the great repository of human ills. Who's to say it isn't, as much as it is that which "flies like a bird" and moves like a stunned deer? Kelly is, among her other selves, a shrewd cartographer of the heart.

Our connection to birds remains to be explored, and Kelly minces no words in making a blistering pronouncement: "We are not birds. Despite our walls covered / With winged men, we are

---

56. Brigit Pegeen Kelly, *Song* and *The Orchard*, "Pipistrelles," Carcanet Press, Ltd. (2008), 44-45.

not birds. / And all that is birdlike in bats / Is also deception."[57] If, as Kelly portends, we operate more like bats than birds through a sort of wounded echolocation, then it follows that "all that is birdlike / In us" is also "illusion."[58] Given her great affection for these, our fine-feathered friends, I can only imagine the severance is heartbreaking, that it begs in her the restoration of at least an avian trace in the poem's final lines: "there is nothing at all of the bird in us... / Except for flight. Except for flight."[59] That final phrase needing, in that moment of dissociation and vulnerability, repetition and reinforcement, and being true enough to drive us into the skies by the billions, and into the skies of feeling wherever the heart opens its wings and flies.

Are we done with birds yet? Almost. In the next poem, "Cry of the Jay," Kelly writes one of the most beautiful sentences—connotatively and visually—I ever saw fly from her pen:

> The sky is not
> so blue or so contained:
> bird breast a cobalt pistol
> shot: the small heart bursting
> into raucous cry:
> the whole packed-in warmth of June focused
> and set free.[60]

The shape of the poem follows, presumptively, the flight of the bird, and the shape of the meaning paints the bird's character to a tee—little brash raucous scoundrel. Note the pistol line extending like a gun's nose. The lines of the heart bursting into cry, then

57. Ibid., 45.
58. Ibid., 45-46.
59. Ibid., 46.
60. Ibid., "Cry of the Jay," 47.

doubling back on itself, the way the urge to sing compels the heart into song until the breath relents and then the heart pumps again to keep the song afloat. The same poem later makes an ontological statement in perfect alignment with my own feeling that we never leave God's—nor Nature's—womb: "Unlimited / gratitude might take such / a shape: *We are within. It is the only place:* Sanctuary of sameness / made strange by hard-hit sight". The last clause clarifies our blindness to this state: hard-hit, we focus on the local, on the woundedness of our person, and over time we lose sight of our being within the Earth and the Divine, and so our host seems strange—if only it to us. The spell to break this self-made jail is gratitude: the affective, embracing outlook that made the poet Robinson Jeffers once declare: "I have fallen in love outward"[61], ancient antidote to ancient—and modern—delirium.

The last thought I'll peck of Kelly's birds is a curious one: "Perhaps God is a bird. Sometimes I think this. The thought / is as good as another." At last, in a simple tautology, she reveals her deity as avian. Then she undercuts the revelation with "sometimes" and the notion that other thoughts are just as good, but those of us who've flown this far with her know to take the sober pronouncement seriously: perhaps what ties us together, even our host, Mother Earth, and all celestial bodies great and small, is movement, is *flight*.

The closing poem in the collection, a seven-page

---

61. Poemhunter.com, https://www.poemhunter.com/poem/the-tower-beyond-tragedy/, accessed December 22nd, 2024.

narrative train that warranted its own section, rivals the book's
first for stature, though "Song" remains the crowd favorite,
which might tell the young poet something about the relative
importance of first and last positions. Eavan Boland called it a
"deceptive, untidy pastoral...wrapped around its own careful
disorder" and judged it the masterpiece of the book.[62] I wouldn't
go that far, but I'd come close: it's very fine, and, as Betty Adcock
said, it's hard to imagine "a better end-piece for the book."[63] The
poem opens at dusk, with a mother and her two children playing
baseball by a cow field with a tennis ball and a stick. Of course,
a Kelly stick is no usual stick, but a limb from a poplar felled by
a hurricane that continued to bloom for two years, flat against
the ground. Nor was the dusk a usual dusk: it "was coming out of
the ground. I heard a poet say this. / The darkness doesn't come
down but rises up. / And he was right. It gets the ankles first."[64]
Good as these details are, lines most poets would love to pen, in
Kelly they're merely scene-setting. The heart of the poem rests
with the cows, who took to playing their own game: "they'd come
/ Together with their flat noses touching, and then // Very slowly
they'd start turning like a wheel." The field steep, the turning
was difficult, but the wheel "moved faster and faster / In ragged

62. Web.Archive.org, https://web.archive.org/web/20180204214252/
http://poems.com/special_features/prose/essay_boland_kelly.php,
accessed May 27th, 2019.
63. Betty Adcock, "Six Soloists," *The Southern Review*, Vol. 32, No. 4
(Fall 1996), 775.
64. Brigit Pegeen Kelly, *Song* and *The Orchard*, "Three Cows and the
Moon," Carcanet Press, Ltd. (2008), 78.

circles. /.../ As if to cover all the ground".[65] A bovine vision that brings to mind crop circles, and just as it approaches the limit of belief, just as the cows approach something they cannot endure, Kelly breaks the tension:

> And then all at once the wheel would shatter,
> The way a wooden wheel shatters when it strikes rock,
> Spokes flying off in all directions. The cows
>
> Would stagger to their corners, shaking their heads.
> And then after awhile they'd make another circle.
> *Sometimes our hearts are stone. Sometimes not.*[66]

Stone: yet another layer to the bird-flying, deer-stunned, domed-dark heart. One of Kelly's brilliant compositional choices for the piece was to stick to event and movement, to seek no verbal explanation where none was likely to be found. And to weave the story of the land and its history in with the story of her family and their experience in the field, continually moving away from and back to the present, Boland's "careful disorder." As the moon rose "it looked like a pale bird moving through the air / That smelled of old batteries, a ghost bird / Beating its wings above the ghost light of the bull's horns",[67] which segues into an older story, of Kelly raising the bull, who had a man's face, and whose mother died after childbirth. The mother died while Kelly slept, making a terrible foghorn sound "like a ship that was going down," the sound breaking into her dream, "about a window that had been shattered by rocks",[68] a dream that spins, while the cows continue

65. Ibid., 78-79.
66. Ibid., 79.
67. Ibid., 80.
68. Ibid., 81.

their own gyrations, dizzyingly from there:

> [...] The window was black and large, and as it

> Opened wider and wider it became the mouth of a lion,
> Out of which something issued, something small,
> Maybe an insect or maybe the hands of a child.[69]

The kaleidoscopic shifting from foghorn to window to lion to preternatural issuance might seem accidental—whatever comes to mind—but Kelly never felt accidental, so it seems to me calculated, or the genesis of a calculation to come. She's spinning us out of the atmosphere—out of the nightmare, the poem, the book—just as a troubling dream does, spinning us to the edge, and then she wakes up. She's also prefiguring numerous such moments in her next book where the "other" world climbs directly into hers, not in a dream, but in waking reality. Given how many through-lines there are across her books, I assume the continuity is long-ripening and intentional.

From dream Kelly returns to the field, starting with the quotidian. The sky brightens at the moment before it goes black. It starts to rain. She and the children quit playing and watch the cows. Then they too are caught up in the strange force that makes them spin. Kelly says "Maybe there were wings. // Maybe the cows had wings under their legs. /.../ Maybe the dark was winged."[70] Her old dream of flight. It gets so dark they cannot see and all whirls. The dark that took their ankles threatens to swallow them up. They touch a poplar for safety, the seer in the field. They fall "toward

69. Ibid.
70. Ibid., 81-82.

the sounds of each other. /.../ Whatever we are without bodies."
Embodiment escapes and surrounds them. There are eyes in the
air, "the sound / of flesh being punched. Of fur being torn." The
nightmare enters the night. "The children's skin pricked by cold //
smelled of bleeding. And blood tastes of cooked flowers."[71] Again
the pitch approaches the unbearable, whence she breaks—nay,
dismantles—the spell:

> And the last sound was the sound of the cows stopping
>
> In the final circle. And it was quiet then.
> And we were looking up. Light flooding a room.
> The four corners of the night all staked out.
>
> The moon high up and small. High up and small.
> Perfect like a flower. Or an oracle. Something
> Completely understood. But unspeakable.[72]

As the tension dissipates, the stillness comes over the family in
waves: first the cows, then the quiet, then the floodlight, then the
moon tucked up neat in the sky, then the floral, and the oracle
of Kelly herself, then understanding, received like the gust of
wind from a single wingbeat, passes from the bird of God or the
unspeakable through her senses. Something so whole, so complete,
the tongue—of the experience, the poem and the book: all three—
stays quiet in the mouth. The understanding something that can
only in its final stages be felt, its resonance ringing the bells of her
cells, the vibration of self become a part of the cosmic hum. Song
has come to an end, and in the course of its being sung, it sent the
winged comet of Brigit Pegeen Kelly flying across the map.

71. Ibid., 83.
72. Ibid.

III: *The Orchard*

Nine years elapsed between *Song* and *The Orchard*, the century turning, Kelly racking up two more spots in *Best American Poetry* and two more Pushcarts, among a host of other recognitions, while continuing to shun the personal limelight. As the commodification of poetry took off and the marketing blitz led to what's now known as PoBiz, Kelly stuck to the work and her private literary citizenship, a model many poets—myself included—could emulate with immense relief. In a memorial article written by former student Ryo Yamaguchi, Yamaguchi says that, with Kelly, "craft was never a lesson but a way of orienting oneself," and that rather than speak of commercial or critical paths to success, "she spoke of poets as people, always, in particular circumstances, with particular pursuits, and success always as something that was, in the end, personally measured."[73] One could apply external validations to a personal measure, or one could construct an inner barometer and test for, say, a deep and abiding satisfaction with the effort one has put into the work, letting the reviews and accolades fall, as they so quickly will, to the gutters. If there's heart in the work and it beats strongly for a long while, what else matters?

Her approach to the business of poetry may have kept to old habits, but her poetry itself continued to evolve. If *Trumpets* saw her testing out and coming into possession of her powers, and if *Song* saw her pushing the dark lyric to one of its limits, *The Orchard* saw her shift away from lyric compression towards narrative fluidity, towards poetry as foreboding fable, which isn't to say it was less dense, but that the old creaky-porch storyteller had fused with and grown into the oracle, had grown through the rocking chair into the bedrock from which she would spin myths so swampy with insinuation—something half-sinister and half-glorious humidifying the air—that one would somehow both shiver and sweat while listening to the tales spun from her lips, threads as wholesome yet harrowing as spider webs or blighted wheat. As Eavan Boland remarked, "*The Orchard*...was a graver, darker enterprise. The poems were less lyrical, the lines longer. Frequently the texts tilted over into heraldic prose arguments."[74]

73. Michigan Quarterly Review online, https://sites.lsa.umich.edu/mqr/2016/11/remembering-brigit-pegeen-kelly-1951-2016/, accessed December 7, 2019.
74. Web.Archive.org, https://web.archive.org/web/20180204214252/http://poems.com/special_features/prose/essay_boland_kelly.php, accessed December 7, 2019.

In her late work, while never really faltering in the mechanics, and while still possessing an unassuming but rock-solid ear, Kelly shifted the focus of the poems further from their internal music towards the clarity of realms so deeply imagined, they come across as embodied, inhabited, lived, endured. Sarah Manguso seemed to agree, deepening the insight with her comment: "these poems pursue clarity at the cost of almost any other principle—a tendency originating from an apparent belief that, by definition, a poem is already infinitely far from the world it describes, and all but doomed to fail in its attempt to make even the smallest authentic sound."[75] I would quibble endlessly with Manguso's limited sense of authenticity, but I agree that the poems are "far," perhaps more "far within" than "far away", or somehow, authentically, both. In any case, again and again in *The Orchard,* I find that Kelly's intent isn't merely to offer a vision, but to build it up and rouse it—living and breathing—around us. To do this, at Kelly's standard, I think one must work from the shoulder of the creator, able to look the creator in the face and ask for guidance, her control so pervasive and penetrating she rarely, if ever, takes a misstep. I'm building this up not only because I think *The Orchard* is her best book, but because it's how the book makes me feel: having endured the staggering force and grace of primal creation.

Like both previous books, *The Orchard* opens with an uppercut, "Black Swan," which doubles as a story she told her son

75. Believermag.com, https://believermag.com/brigit-pegeen-kel-lys-the-orchard/, accessed December 7, 2019.

about how she found him, before he was hers, sleeping under a bush beside a black swan, and a story about the intricate, winding paths of creation that double back on themselves in great, crisscrossing loops. Kelly's old friend the goat has a cameo where "the bush's hot white flowers [smelled] / As rank and sweet as the stewed milk of a goat," and her beloved birds can be heard crying "in every bush / And bed." [76] Kelly's territory is, despite its strangeness, as familiar as ever, though it, like most of her poems, seem to occupy "a place / So old it seemed to exist outside of time." Often, one could forget that Kelly was writing from the Midwest, extracting its hidden depths, or, as former student Amie Whittmore put it, "she squeezed the rag of that dull landscape till it spit out all its secrets."[77] If secrets were coal, Kelly would be their expert miner. "Black Swan" is an intriguing genesis story, especially in how, watching her son sleeping with the swan, "his arm around the swan's moist neck," "the feathered breast and the bare breast breathing as one," she:

> very swiftly and without making a sound,
> So that I would not wake the sleeping bird,
> I picked the boy up and slipped him into my belly,
> The way one might slip something stolen
> Into a purse.[78]

A highly original and startling take: if it's been done before—

76. Brigit Pegeen Kelly, *Song* and *The Orchard*, "Black Swan," Carcanet Press, Ltd. (2008), 89.
77. Amiewhittemore.com, https://amiewhittemore.com/2016/10/20/remembering-brigit-pegeen-kelly/, accessed December 7, 2019.
78. Brigit Pegeen Kelly, *Song* and *The Orchard*, "Black Swan," Carcanet Press, Ltd. (2008), 89.

motherhood as thievery—(it probably has), I haven't seen it. Kelly could stop there and surprise us, but she presses on: despite the story being nearly unforgettable, she herself forgets its world until her son, accosted by bullies at school, reminds her, saying "I wish I had never / Been born. I wish I were back under the bush," a heartbreaking wish, but also one that revives the old world and their pre-history together. The old world renews, but it has shifted, for this time, when the garden rises around her, the swan is missing, and ominous horses approach, their "giant stone hooves... / striking and striking the hardening ground,"[79] which could be the hardening of the boy's heart, of her's against his tormenters, or much mysterious else—made more alluring by leaving the rest for us to imagine, or perhaps to pick up from that moment in another poem.

The second poem, "Blessed Is the Field," returns us to Kelly's floral realm, where growth and decay continue their work as fertility's cooperative halves: "the steaming flowers, green and gold, / The acid-bitten leaves....".[80] Where singing itself is bittersweet: the singing sweet, though "the words / do not always seem to work", and sweetbitter, for: "the insect's song both magnifies / The field and casts a shadow over it". In her more hopeful moments, Kelly tries to find the grace in suffering's grip: "*Blessed is the day. And the one // Who destroys the day. Blessed is the ring of fire / In which we live....*". Blessed are we, even while cursed, though at times the

79. Ibid., 90.
80. Ibid., "Blessed Is the Field," 91.

blessing becomes burdensome to carry; we may eat "self-heal, / Humblest of flowers," and it may not work; we may "not get well" but the eating "may [still] strike // your fancy."[81] The glimmer of the possibility of getting better is enough to carry us forward, even if the glimmer fades and we come to recognize that "goldenrod is the color // Of beaten skin." Hard the life of being beaten, but having existed before the beating and existing after—even during—we may find the strength to "say: *Blessed are those who stand still / in their confusion. Blessed is the field as it burns.*" The blessing is no less present for suffering's continual plunge and twist of the knife into the heart.

Most of *The Orchard* is a narrative affair, but there's one shining exception in "Black Legs," a poem so lyrical it's nearly impossible to paraphrase—one of the keystone signs of great work—and I'd rate it in her top five. Ostensibly about a boy and a few animals, it reminds me of "The Music Lesson," with the unassuming subject of a boy taking piano lessons. The poem opens with a childish, fairytale logic:

> The sheep has nipples, the boy said,
> And fur all around. The sheep
> Has black legs, his name is Blacklegs
> And a cry like breaking glass.
> The glass is broken. The glass
> Is broken, and the milk falls down.[82]

The boy's mind associates freely, forming a cluster of characteristics by which Blacklegs becomes distinct from the other sheep, namely

81. Ibid., 92.
82. Ibid., "Blacklegs," 95.

his leg coloring and the glass-breaking timbre of his cry, which brings to mind a small trouble, potentially large in the mind of a child, of a milk glass breaking, the milk falling from the table, a punishment to follow, which could compel one to wonder: what did Blacklegs do to be born with such a cry? Then the boy expands his small bestiary, marking a bee by its "suffering softness", its "ring of fur / Like a ring of fire" and saying it "burns / the flowers he enters, the way / The rain burns the grass." Marking, too, a horse by the way "he holds a moon... / In his mouth, cups it like water / So it will not spill out." What could this be—the moon of his teeth, or a white tongue? Up to now, the poem reads like a curious glimpse into the mind of a child, but then the register shifts:

> And the boy said this. I am a boy
> And a man. My legs are two,
> And they shine black as the arrows
> That drop down on my throat
> And my chest to draw out the blood
> The bright animals feed on,
> Those with wings, those without,
> The ghosts of the heart—whose
> Hunger is a dress for my song.[83]

Now the speaker reveals that he's a man, either early in manhood or never having lost his boyishness, and his legs are black like the sheep's, and what's more, he's a ghost whose throat and chest were torn open by arrows, perhaps the arrowed legs of another sheep, and his wounds are sources of nourishment where the winged and wingless alike come to feed, in life and perhaps even after, haunting the heart, "whose / Hunger is a dress for my song." This

---

83. Ibid., 95-96.

woundedness brings us back to "The Place of Trumpets" in her first book, "Where the wound loves the arrow",[84] and to "Botticelli's St. Sebastian" in *Song*, where the heart, a stunned deer, moves through the woods and the trees close over it like "a lasting wound".[85] The wound as feeding site furthers her attempt to find grace in the worst of circumstances, and it places another piece of the puzzle of the heart together; along with its stoniness, its flightiness, its stunnedness and its domed dark—its *hunger*, the thing to which we are inescapably beholden, drives and "dresses" her song. A hunger that others will eat from, like we eat from her poems and the heart of which she made them. To fully paraphrase the poem feels impossible, which reminds me of Archibald MacLeish's dictum, "A poem should not mean / But be."[86] Certainly, Kelly's poems *are,* and they weigh heavy in the depth and density of their being. But I think MacLeish is only half right. A poem can mean *and* be, and Kelly's capable of doing both.

Increasingly, one of the traits I find most admirable in Kelly is her ability to subvert expectations. Give her a sheep's filthy neck and she sees it as "honey to the flies. Rancid honey. Each coarse curl dipped in it."[87] Give her a goat in one poem and he steals the show. Give her a goat in another, a goat "who pounded his head

84. Brigit Pegeen Kelly, *To the Place of Trumpets*, "The Place of Trumpets," Yale University Press (1988), 65.
85. Brigit Pegeen Kelly, *Song* and *The Orchard*, "Black Swan," Carcanet Press, Ltd. (2008), 69.
86. Archibald MacLeish, *Collected Poems 1917-1982*, "Ars Poetica," Houghton Mifflin (1985), 107.
87. Brigit Pegeen Kelly, *Song* and *The Orchard*, "Sheep Child," Carcanet Press, Ltd. (2008), 100.

against a tree / Until he was dead" and all she says is that "his name was Bumblebee...",[88] as though the story weren't worth continuing. And yet she's not just being subversive for subversiveness's sake. She's keeping us on our toes, sure, but it's in the service of teasing out the thousand ways a thing is, those innumerable intersecting angles, so few of which we get to witness. Moss on the statue of a lion "blood[ies] her small feet."[89] The ground is the ground, but also: "the ground is a flock of dead birds."[90] Stillness is an illusion, movement carries all—Kelly could see the lie of inanimacy as easily as she could see into the heart of a statue.

Much of her vocation in poetry, I think, is the art and act of attention. A holy art, for in one sense, attention is all we have, or the most of what we can give that couldn't be given by anyone else. Attention and the emotion we imbue it with. Attention and care. A spiritual art and physical act. A practice of illumination and revelation, of seeing and digging, beholding the soul and turning the soil, holding up what she finds. This essay is, in part, an attempt to turn and marvel at the art of her attentiveness in my hands. An attentiveness that looks back at me. Let me tell you a few of the things I see.

First is the way her attentiveness peels back the layers of presence. Typically focused on animals and atmospheres, in "Brightness from the North" she changes tack and takes on time: "it seems as if / this might be what forever is, the presence of

88. Ibid.
89. Ibid., "The South Gate," 102.
90. Ibid.

time / Overriding the body of time, the fullness of time / Not a moment but a being, watchful and unguarded".[91] The day and the hour blend into a single continuous being who bears creatures and events, a turn of mind that squares with quantum physicists' notion that phenomena don't happen in time, they exude it, forming and reforming and in their motion creating an appearance of duration. A reformation known as embodiment itself. As Kelly puts it, "We can say, we can say your body / Appeared on the table, and swiftly disappeared— /.../ and the ground / Took the body, and the ground was pleased."[92] That the ground took the body it gave up in pleasure might seem like a stretch to us who try to claim pleasure for ourselves, but anything of ours was first Mother Earth's, is always Earth's, so who's to say she doesn't feel pleasures we can't discern? Planetary pleasures that include pleasures known to humans. She took the body after she took to the body in the first place. The point isn't to believe in nonsense, but to entertain the possibility and recognize that, limited in our knowledge, enswaddled in mystery, we can't but taste the vast strangenesses swirling around and within us, and articulating new tastes of strangeness is one of Kelly's most visceral gifts.

Second in her holy art of attention is her ability to animate, or to invoke the animism pervading the so-called dead and the so-called unliving in the form of statuary. *Unseeing the lie of inanimacy.* In "The South Gate", a stone lion's "stained breasts [are] suddenly

91. Ibid., "Brightness from the North," 98.
92. Ibid.

/ full of milk," dripping, with "no one / to catch the liquid as it falls, sweet and fast, / to the ground", with "Moss on the lion's legs. Moss / bloodying her small feet."[93] Poor lion: bloodied with no one to drink her milk, or is there? In the "corner / of her deformed head a dream lodges", the dream of a child, a child in the ground, which "is a flock of dead birds." A curdling dream: the lion's milk feeds the ground where a dead no-one (who might become again a someone) drinks it and "stirs. Soon he will stagger from / burial. Terrible. Wrapped in soiled cloth. / Stinking. Lion flesh and bird flesh and man flesh", which is to say that all the fleshes feeding the Earth, the dead birds and the milk and our own corpses, comingle and rise in the terrible body of a statue's child. Of each child. It's a shiversome thing to behold, a dead-and-resurrected-forth story, found and brought to light all because the stained breasts of the stone lion offered Kelly their portal, and because she possesses the uncanny ability to bring the slightest suggestions into the fullest living expression.

Third in her art of attention is her keen observation of, and willingness to expose, the inner life—difficult, sorrowful, often kept quiet, under wraps. In "Rose of Sharon," our old, floral friend from book one who will be by Kelly's side until the end, Kelly begins with her affection for the bush, how she "would have loved it / For its name alone", and continues to admire its qualities—"its fleshy blossoms. How fat they were. How fast they fell"—including its attendant spirits, "the doves / Mean as spit, [who] fought the

93. Ibid., "The South Gate," 102.

finches and the sparrows / for the golden seed I spilled beneath the bush."[94] But the meanness isn't theirs alone, for she "threw seed just to watch the birds fight", a perverse pleasure, difficult but honorable to admit. She loved the bush until "An ice storm felled the tree," loved it still, despite "The breasts gone dry. The window opening onto / Bare grass. The small birds waiting / For the seed I do not throw," and loved it further, fretting over its final days: "Did the bush fear the ice? [...] Did its featherweight nature darken / Just before it was felled?" It was the *"Pride of my heart,"* she says, a friend she could lose, but not let go.

The inner life: her work of mapping the heart, one of her most persistent endeavors in the books. In "Elegy," she says, "the heart moves as the moths do, scuttering / Like a child's thoughts above this broken stone / And that."[95] How keenly observed: that the heart, while having a knack for passion and single-minded perseverance, isn't always so whole and collected. Sometimes it's a shaking, arthritic, weak-fingered grasping, a flimsy composite of many weary, life-bludgeoned parts. Sometimes it's a ruptured, disorderly dispersal, desperately seeking the light on any mothwing, even if the light will singe its wings and burn it out of flight. The heart hoofs and flies, is the pulsing gamut and the void, the throat underfoot and the body one betroths, the presence of all creation that's sometimes barely there, the euphoria of fondness itself on one day, then fond of nothing, wanting to die. And

94. Ibid., "Rose of Sharon," 110.
95. Ibid., "Elegy," 115.

"holding someone's heart in your hands", no matter how much you love them, and they you, is like trying to "hold a cloud of moths."[96] The same for oneself. The feeling of the fluttering, in the good moments, outweighs the inability to grasp it. The heart is strong; it is weak; it protects; it self-destructs; it enshrines a body of ethics; it rebels and obeys no laws. These are some of things I see, and that see me, when I turn Kelly's art within my hands, hands which remind me that much of my life belongs to them.

One could continue to enumerate Kelly's kinds and degrees of attention, and there are many more to be explored in her work, but I'd like to leave that to the pleasures of personal discovery and shift the focus towards the function of narrative in the book. In one manner, it makes the poems less uneven, approaches flawlessness, partially because narrative tends to be more entertaining and more forgiving than lyric, but more so because Kelly's meditative powers were so concentrated, so convincing, that to read her late tales is less to listen than to live them. Another aspect of their brilliance is that she doesn't recast myth the way scores of poets and historians do; she listens to the mythic weight of her perceptions and creates her own. Sadly, many of them are too long to quote in full, but one, "Pale Rider," begins with a dead doe she found in the woods, its legs cut off, killed out of season. Months later, on a walk through the oldest part of the woods, she encountered something in the air that her mind refused to understand, until it clearly became the doe's face, appearing and disappearing in the mist, multiplying until it

96. Ibid.

was "four heads on four long necks, / Attached to one legless body, one golden swollen body / That smelled of fallen fruit splitting in the sun and shone / The way an image from a dream will darkly shine."[97] Except that it wasn't a dream, or no more so than reality is, with all its unbelievable encounters, whence an upside-down head emerged from the doe's chest, a child, its body still embedded in its mother's, as it was in the legless corpse Kelly first encountered. The story gets eerier and hairier from there, ending with Kelly "lost in the woods where...I stood / In the dark until I closed my eyes. And then I stood no more",[98] her own presence as ephemeral as the rest. Her own presence ripe with the power to return, a woman who became mist in the midst of being human. In the midst of the deer, her personal guide and portal to the realms that bleed into ours.

Two more in this vein, "The Dragon" and "The Foreskin," seem to me as close to brief acts of sorcery as words can come. In the former, a poem that grips me as forcefully as "Song," two swarms of bees "the size of melons" come "out of the junipers", carrying a snake between them:

> Lifting each side of his narrow neck, just below
> The pointed head, and in this way, very slowly
> They carried the snake through the garden,
> The snake's long body hanging down, its tail dragging
> The ground, as if the creature were a criminal
> Being escorted to execution or a child king
> To the throne.[99]

97. Ibid., "Pale Rider," 118.
98. Ibid., 120.
99. Ibid., "The Dragon," 125.

At first, she "kept thinking the snake / Might be a hose," until she

saw:

> [...] his body green as the grass
> His tail divided, his skin oiled, the way the male member
> Is oiled by the female's juices, the greenness overbright,
> The bees gold, the winged serpent moving silently
> Through the air. There was something deadly in it,
> Or already dead. Something beyond the report
> Of beauty.[100]

Beauty seems to me an odd choice of word for such an otherworldly

scene, but I believe it was beautiful in the act of composition,

and beyond beautiful in creation's aftermath. How could it not

be? It takes a creator's eye to carve such careful details: the slow

reportage of the procession, the scenery and specimens alive at the

tip of her pen, bringing with them a realm which may, as it turns

out, not be so otherworldly.

When some former students once visited Kelly at her

home, "she showed them a sculpture of a dog and described the

time a swarm of bees emerged from its mouth,"[101] which raises all

sorts of questions about how grounded in experiences her "myths"

are. In any case, at this point in "The Dragon," having witnessed

the winged serpent, Kelly presses her face to her arm and leaves

it there, as if in disbelief or overcome with despair, while the bees

carry out their mission. I'm not keen to suggest a psychological

correlative to her poem, but it's almost unheard of for Kelly to turn

away from a vision—her normal response is to gaze unflinching into

---

100. Ibid.
101. Medium.com, https://medium.com/@coreymiller/remember-ing-brigit-pegeen-kelly-569124086ce6, accessed December 9, 2019.

its darkest pit—so it seems to me quite possible that something in her own past or person was being carried through the vision and out, for in its wake, when she "looked up":

> [...] the bees and the snake were gone,
> But the garden smelled of broken fruit, and across
> The grass a shadow lay for which there was no source,
> A narrow plinth dividing the garden, and the air
> Was like the air after a fire, or the air before a storm,
> Ungodly still, but full of dark shapes turning.[102]

This is the state of the cleansed, the purified, the transformed or the soon-to-be. It's also the state I find myself in after being possessed by the best of her poems. As Carl Phillips said, "perhaps the best way to describe" Kelly's work might be the final lines,[103] which I'll quote again to consider in this new light:

> [...] and the air
> Was like the air after a fire, or the air before a storm,
> Ungodly still, but full of dark shapes turning.[104]

Indeed, there's a chilling portrait of her overall artistry in that fearsome constellation.

The prose poem "The Foreskin" deserves exploration at equal length (no pun intended), a poem about planting her son's foreskin beneath a magnolia after having it removed, but in the interest of leaving another surprise for readerly adventure, let me simply quote a middle sentence, to marvel at how much her gaze could elicit from the "little curl of skin":

---

102. Brigit Pegeen Kelly, *Song and The Orchard*, "The Dragon," Carcanet Press, Ltd. (2008), 125.
103. Poets.org, https://poets.org/text/surreal-no-less-real-brigit-pegeen-kelly, accessed December 8, 2019.
104. Brigit Pegeen Kelly, *Song and The Orchard*, "Sheep Child," Carcanet Press, Ltd. (2008), 100.

> The little curl was pinkish, like an overbred white rabbit's eyes,
> and yellowing white, like the petals of the magnolia blooms,
> and a soft blue; and it had a crust of red, for no one had washed it,
> those who might have done so unprepared for the request for it,
> so they handed it over in its sullied form, which made it, I thought,
> more beautiful.[105]

Imagine if she was writing a poem about his entire body. Her gaze elicits a depth of being as much as it does a depth of meaning. Perhaps even more so. I envy the power of her gaze, but then I doubt the intelligence of the envy. I wouldn't want Kelly's eyes forever—I think they would scare me—but from time to time, I'd have liked to borrow them for a spell. Who's to say that possibility has ended? Perhaps I might earn the right to borrow them still.

As we begin to exit Kelly's haunting, mysterious garden, there are, it seems to me, two major poems towards the close of her book, one of which feels like a consummation of themes and obsessions she spent her career exploring, and one of which reads like the dissolution of her poetry, a strange thing to encounter in what became her final book. The first poem is "The Dance," another long fable in which a sick dog (recall the run-over dog from *Trumpets*), "pathetic...ugly as sin...her fur going white...her dugs...swollen...disfigured...full of rot and not milk"[106] approached, in agonizing fashion—what else—a giant, beautiful statue. Underneath the stone man, the dog sat, and from her mouth crawled a living man, Kelly recounting every gory advance of his body from hers, after which "the dog lay like a castaway coat / to

105. Ibid., "The Foreskin," 126.
106. Ibid., "The Dance," 135.

the side",[107] not dead but spent, and at that moment the stone man

bent over to take a closer look. And the living man, who resembled

the stone man:

> [...] did something like a little dance, assuming one still
> Pose after another, his muscles tight as stones, and the light
> Around him laughing ha ha ha ha ha ha, not in amusement
> But in deep pleasure, the crow laughing ha ha ha ha ha ha,
> And the handsome cypresses spinning like dreidels...[108]

At last the living and the dead and the statuary, the wonder and

the horror and the humor, conflate and converge, each of them

reflected like secret aspects of the other: the world came to life

through and upon stone; the living built their castles through

and upon the dead; the dead keep circling and responding to the

Earth's call: *embody, get up, dance.* And all of us are locked in the

existential hunger that is a "dress for my song," all of us feeding from

one another's wounds, all of us being fed upon as contributions

to creation. This is why the man dances, why the man is being

danced—for:

> [...] Things
> Will be fed on. The rose is fed on by blight, a white ghost,
> And by beetles, tiny green stones, and the calf dead for a week
> Behind the far wall is fed on by vultures, and the bending stone
> Statue is fed on by the rain and the wind—they vie for his eyes,
> His fruit—and the man dances for this, for the devouring.[109]

It's rare that Kelly lays out a reason for why things happen, perhaps

because they rarely come to her purposed from the mist, perhaps

because she's always pushing, pushing and rarely reaches what feels

---

107. Ibid., 136.
108. Ibid.
109. Ibid.

like a mystery-containing vantage, the touchpoint of answer from which the world rebounds, but now she has, the reason reveals itself, so she states it plainly—to feed and be fed on and dance "for the devouring"—then she begins the arduous journey back:

> [...] And now the man's time
> Is up. The figure on the pillar breathes in and draws back
> To his stone state, and the man below sits down and struggles
> To pull on the suit of rag and bone, the man growing smaller
> As the suit grows larger, the dog's mouth at last closing over
> The crown of the man's head, and the poor dog laboring
> To her feet, and beginning again her slow walk, up and on,
> In and out of the shadows, her head swinging from side to side,
> As if she were divining for water. She will walk all the way
> Around the world, until she comes back to the circle of stone,
> And the dance is repeated.[110]

The cycle is ghastly, enlivening, beautiful and terrible—"beyond the report of beauty", but beyond the report of terror? I think no, then I think so, and I circle round from those two poles. We are made by the cycle and undone by the cycle—remade and undone, undone and remade—and no matter what happens, the cycles carry on, disturbing but rarely disturbed, the smaller cycles subsumed in the larger cycles that made them.

There's a hyphenated aside in the middle of the poem that, in the context of Kelly's oeuvre, offers us, I think, another clue to the inner workings of her imagination:

> [...]—and oh, yes,
> It is carried, night a little creature carried by the day, day's child,
> A disfigured creature, and then night grown full, and day carried,
> A beautiful creature, night's child, a white mewling thing
> Like a rose—[111]

---

110. Ibid., 136-137.
111. Ibid., 136.

Everywhere in Kelly wafts this sense of nesting, of cycles, of life within death within stone, and day within night, night within day, beauty within whatever the senses receive and are able to speak, and something beyond beauty in what they receive but can't voice, and I find it curious that stone occupies such centrality in this, not only in that all life anchors therein, but that it's where writing, e.g., cuneiform, and the rules of conduct, e.g., the commandments, were formed. And it seems to me that Kelly's use of statuary in her dark, complex interplay is an argument for art as a living, breathing component of life and existence, not separate therefrom, that the statue doesn't mimic life but carries it, reveals itself as continuous with the life of the artist, even after the artist expires, for life wasn't the artist's, nor the statue's—life is the making and unmaking and remaking: the active force which hammers us and conducts our hands as they write the poems, and guides the sculptor's hands as they unearth the eyes from within the stone: life, and more than life—beyond life—movement: the essential, creative being to which we belong.

This feels to me like a natural resting place, but Kelly is Kelly, and by now, we know better. The final poem in the book, like the final poem in *Song*, is a long single-section piece that marks a turn for her in several ways. Note the form, which, first, ditches her beloved stichic for a seven-page sentence scattered in uneven stanzas, which, second, break as if at the moments where the artist relinquishes or loses control—Kelly's control *was* exquisite—and lays bare the grappling of attention with the world that will give up any number of secrets if pressed hard enough, but never anything close to all it contains. The book—her last book—ends with her beloved birds and deer. "The Sparrow's Gate" opens:

> And the bird shot through, who, had the stone arms been intact,
> would have dashed his small brains out and fallen like a bloody
> cloth to the grass—
>
> the bird shot through—
>
> and the absence, the missing arms beneath the beautiful slope of the
> woman's shoulders, her perpetual *at ease*, the woman not
> requiring as the man might the order to relax—[112]

Thus begins her long circuitous tale which, unlike "Three Cows and the Moon," and unlike most of *The Orchard*, and unlike most of Kelly for that matter, shatters the narrative thread, picking it up only to lose it again, as if trying to catch the sparrow in her hands and finding that her hands are there in appearance only, or trying to catch the shape of a thought only for it to disappear at the strike of attention. Absence is a key word, and turns out to be the subject she's trying to pin down. Though of course she can't, for it's the hole that has no consistent shape nor place nor meaning, and no matter what she feeds it, it does not grow full, it does not appear, its hunger hungers more—it grows ever larger with ever more things and beings to eat. It won't tilt over into a presence she can apprehend, even though it exhibits presence-like characteristics. It exists not as some phenomenon, an existent, but as existence itself—all phenomena and none.

    In one tack, she tries to imagine the life of the woman, but

112. Ibid., "The Sparrow's Gate," 143.

that doesn't work, so she takes to cataloguing everything the absence

is not, and there she shines. A few snippets:

> not the sparrow's foolhardy bravura that blasted him safely past the
> woman's breast and into the trees, only to impale him soon
> after on the hound's blunt tooth;
>
> [...]
>
> not the terrible draining at the center of the day when the spirit
> topples like a statue to the grass
>
> [...]
>
> not a single sheet of paper, a letter whose words no matter how
> rearranged are a dark glass held up before the world upon
> which one can rap and rap and get no answer;
>
> not that rapping;
>
> none of it, no:[113]

And when that doesn't work either, she retraces her steps:

> If you lie on the grass in the dead of summer, and sleep, your body
> heavier than stone, and wake to the sound of something
> tapping and tapping like a sculptor's tool on stone, and look up
> from your dream to see a sparrow hurtling like a missile past
> the stone woman's left breast, right where the arm would have
> been,[114]

Kelly herself becomes the statue woken by the sculptor's tap, and

again tries to grapple with absence's tidal feeling: something missing

and something going away. After a series of if statements, she begins,

at last, to gain purchase on it, perhaps her focus on the-won't-be

accruing to her a means by which to focus on the-was: "then the

absent arms are so heavy; /.../ with the heaviness of something at

anchor:" A heaviness that explodes her into another catalogue, but

113. Ibid., 144-146.
114. Ibid., 146.

this one more personal, this one populated by the flora and fauna that have appeared and reappeared like omens, totems, portals, powers and presences in her work—the birds, the deer, the carp, the lambs, the hounds, the fruit:

> all the imaginings, sweet god, the many arms of the mind, the
> many-mindedness of the spirit descending upon itself, making
> a fullness that seeks entrance and when entrance is found
> unable—like water driven up from below—to resist the
> opening, and so it shoots out, a blossoming of sparrows gone
> mad, making a blessing[115]

Here we come to the heart of things: absence won't be held, won't stop draining us, but in the making of absence, the whole teeming, pulsing "many-mindedness of the spirit" lives and knows itself through us, and to witness this, to love and suffer it, is the making of our blessing and our horror, and this poem reads to me like the soft, helpless, grateful poem of a poet bidding her beloved apparitions goodbye. A reminder that as we face the absence of Kelly, and Kelly's work, the absence needn't forever be grieved as loss, for the forms are not lost, but changed.

And so we reach the end of Kelly's last book, but not, I think, the end of her tale. Though the books and the poems—with a handful of post-*Orchard* exceptions—have swept underfoot. And though turning back won't give us the versions of the poems, the versions of world and self we met and made in first encounter, it will give us the deepening of second encounters, and third. During one such encounter—don't ask me how many, I lost count—it occurred to me that there's one more matter to be explored:

115. Ibid., 148.

whether Kelly knew the end of her work was coming and took an active hand in shaping its closure. For most poets, this would seem preposterous—she lived twelve more years, and died relatively young at sixty-five—but for Kelly, whose work was so careful, whose control was so masterful, whose architecture from beginning to end fit together in numerous nesting and crescendoing ways, I think there's a chance that she both sensed and participated in the finality, as if each of the books, and each of the poems, was a brushstroke in a larger painting. I don't mean that she planned it out or mapped into the books some hermetic design, and I have no sense that she was more conscious than un- about their final weaving, but certain evidence leads to believe that perhaps she felt the silence—the absence—rising up and gave it voice—that she used its paint as she had with everything else that crossed her palette.

My first clue comes late in the long narrative, "Pale Rider," where she says "and I thought / Of the tongue, of how it is a wound, a pool of blood, / and of how you should bind a wound." [116] As we saw before, Kelly's wounds were sites of nourishment, both for those who feed from them and for those who are thereby given the opportunity to appreciate being wounded: *the wound loves the arrow*. And yet, depending on the depth and severity of the wound, if one wishes to remain alive, one *should* bind it. I can't help but think there's a subtle suggestion here, if not admission, of the need to bind the wound of poetry, lest it bleed too much. Who

116. Ibid., "Pale Rider," 119.

knows what the poems required of her? Certainly not me, but I know that just to read them is, while emphatically pleasurable and addictive, also at times to undergo a trial. And as a poet I can easily begin to feel myself crushed by the proposition of composing more. Of working at that pitch of fever, maintaining self and sanity while plumbing the edges of an almost-madness. I hope this isn't true—I hope they were a joy to her and a labor of love—but given their recurring darkness, I cannot help but wonder.

My second clue comes in the very next poem, "Masque," which offers a harrowing scene:

> My foot bleeds on the rocks
> Of the shallow stream. The crows
> Thick above me and at their backs
> The larger gravebirds. This
> Is a mean task, this business
> Of burying oneself before one
> Is dead. The shovel always
> Breaks, the weather worsens,
> The spot chosen proves to be
> The wrong spot, and the words,
> The words of mercy one must
> Mutter, possess no mercy
> For the flesh[117]

After having the thought that the tongue should be bound, the wound of the tongue cauterized, she seems to actively take up the work of burying herself before she died. What self could she be burying? The poet? Perhaps. It could also be the personal self, the ego in its attempt to impose ownership on the forces that move her. I suspect there's at least a little of both being entombed in the endeavor. Burying an aspect of oneself is a *mean* task, but

---

117. Ibid., "Masque," 121.

also exceedingly difficult, as the breaking shovel, the worsening
weather, the wrong words, and the inadequacy of mercy to assuage
the flesh of the gravedigger, all attest. The end of the poem pushes
the flirtation with the thought of relinquishment directly over the
edge (italics mine):

> [...] My crow,
> My lark, my winsome wren,
> My chough, oh sweet-lipped one
> *Who keeps me to a task*
> *I do not want*, let me be more
> Than a dove-witted fool. The light
> Strikes down between the trees.
> The shovel strikes dirt. If the seam
> Is good. If the seam is good. Then
> The heart will put on for a moment
> Its royal robes and become a grave man
> Standing before an open crypt
> With an air of such command
> The stained burial wrappings
> Of one much loved, and maligned,
> And many days dead, will drop
> Away. The self step blind
> From its watery grave. And there
> Will be: No time. Nor crow.
> Nor Lazarus. Nor Christ.
> *Nor the hand that writes this.*[118]

One could read "a task / I do not want" as momentary—sometimes
the muse arrives when she isn't wanted—but when the heart itself,
one of Kelly's great subjects, drops away into an open grave, and
the self steps blind from it, missing "the hand that writes this," it
seems to me that Kelly senses herself on the edge of, and may even
invite, putting down the pen: being reborn.

     If there's any truth to this, I like to think of it as a
lightening, as transformational, or as perhaps earning her own

118. Ibid., 121-122.

pair of sparrow's wings, though I'd imagine she'd put it in a more somber tone, something like the following, from "Plants Fed On by Fawns":

> The flies do not trouble me. They are like the stars
> At night. Common and beautiful. They are like
> My thoughts. I stood at midnight in the orchard.
> There were so many stars, and yet the stars,
> The very blackness of the night, though perfectly
> Cold and clear, seemed to me to be insubstantial,
> The whole veil of things seemed less substantial
> Than the thing that moved in the dark behind me,
> An unseen bird or beast, something shifting in its sleep,
> Half-singing and then forgetting it was singing:
> *Be thou always ravished by love*[119]

Perhaps her outgrowth was fitting, deserved. Having taken both the lyric and the narrative to their respective limits, limits which scores of poets from all camps achingly admire, where could she go from there? Drama, perhaps, but no, there was plenty of drama in her poems. Sometimes, with decades of writing behind me, I sense the glimmer of a poetic movement, a movement of the mind and heart that sheds the need for words, like an old snakeskin or a set of feathers that no longer suit one's current capacity for flight, and I like to think that this is what happened to Kelly, that the poetry took up residence in her blood and buried the pulpit of her tongue. Yes, if there's any truth to this, I like to think of that dark movement, the one she sensed under every feather and statue and doe, sneaking up on her one night, relieving the burden of her gift, and yet still singing its darkness through her, still imbuing her every cell and sense with a living poetry, a poetry that could, in

---

119. Ibid., "Plants Fed On by Fawns," 131.

return for all she gave, grant her moments of *unlimited gratitude,* a

poetry that could, without cease and without the need for words,

grant her to *be always ravished by love.*

IV: Last Poems

Of course, Kelly wasn't done yet: *The Orchard* was her last book, but it wasn't her last published poem. I, too, thought I was done with this book, that it was right to end on a dark, earned, ravishing love, an embodiment of poetry, but it turns out that the book wasn't done with me. Nor was Kelly. I completed the prior sections four years ago, and I knew Kelly had published one more well-known poem—"Iskandariya"—but I didn't know there were four others lurking until four days ago. A new angle of research revealed them at just the right time, as I was preparing this child to meet the world. Four years, four poems, four days. Is this a sign? Is a Kellyean poetics at work in these circumstances? In these thoughts as they occur to me? Perhaps. I'm inclined to think so, but it would be folly to pretend to know.

The pertinent question is: *should I continue*: to which the heart thumps a resounding *yes*. Very well, then—let's walk some more.

I don't think these last poems are common knowledge, despite Kelly's wide, adoring audience. Maybe two of the five. A Google search for one of them, "Geisblatt," turns up three total sources. Three, on the whole know-it-all internet, for a poem from a god-tier poet published in *The Yale Review*, the poem publicly shared for all to see. How is this secrecy possible? Another sign, or at least a nudge that I should do my part to help them find loving hearts and homes. To even know they exist feels, just now, like being back in the field where a deer's head emerges from the misty air, emerges not to speak, not to tell me something, but to initiate me into its realm. A deer that isn't just a deer.

I was looking back over Kelly's titles and noticed that the penultimate poem in *Song* is called "All Wild Animals Were Once Called Deer." I thought the title was a portal. A token of her love for the species and the archetypes at work in deerly wandering. It *is* a portal. It's also a *truth* I hadn't grasped. In a response to a review of Kelly's work by Fiona Sampson, Tony Cooper noted that, "Kelly is spot on: the Old English word "deor"—which has come down to us as "deer"—could refer to any animal and not simply the tribe of Bambi."[120] A revelation that sends me bounding—quick as a yearling—back over the pages of Kelly's work. Another layer to attend to: thank you, Tony. A layer that reminds me there are many

---

120. Tony Cooper, "Review: Letters: Deer Stalking," *The Guardian* (March 1st, 2008), 15.

more. More layers, more selves, more lives. A book isn't dead. Not after one reading. Not after a hundred. It's an energetic force larger than life, larger than death. My relationship with her books isn't dead either. We grow together, apart, together again—we evolve: I lose memories of her work and the books help me make new ones; I recall old ones in the ground and the books help me bring them back to life: the deer's head newly risen to summon the old affections. I'm grateful.

The deer, which I know now is *animalis* itself, turns, is unmade as deer, remade as another creature, as creaturely making and movement. A creature I cannot see beyond its outline against the light. Its silhouette feels familiar. Then I know it: it's the shadow animal invoked by Kelly's name at the very beginning of this book, wrapping now a feathery wing around my ankles. For what? I can't tell yet. I can only say it's startling and needs to happen. I'm a little afraid but I kind of like it. Then the wing reveals its purpose: to pull me towards the realm of Kelly's last poems. I'm hesitant, afraid of what I might find there. Of what might happen to the love I have for her work as I trace her final steps. Final steps are often hindered or gruesome, pathetic, sad. The fear shutters my eyes. I linger in the darkness. Over-linger. If my dog Addie were here, she'd sense my hesitation, nudge my hand with a nose-push of bravery, and accompany me into the realm. Maybe her ghost is already there, waiting for me to join her. Join the deer. The deer includes her, includes me. I hear her bark and I'm ready now: my eyes open, with

a many-minded spirit—me, Addie, deer, Kelly, shadow animal—
seeing through them.

Five poems. First: "Iskandariya," published in 2005 in the
New York Times. Iskandariya, the Arabic pronunciation of Alexandria,
where knowledge burned. The poem is another prose incancation in
Orchard style, but there's a loosening at play here: looser rhetoric, a
conversational tone, the images still turning imagination into a wet,
felt reality, but not quite so jammed up against one another: pressed
and unpressed, like an accordion or pair of lungs, which require some
space, a little breathing room after all the hard work of tending to
The Orchard. The poem would feel almost at home in that garden,
but seems to me perfectly placed outside the garden gates, waving
farewell, her face already turning away.

A farewell which is also an entrance, passage into a new
portal. Perhaps that's why I didn't want to write about the poem
before. It felt less like an addendum to *The Orchard* than a new
beginning, a departure. "Iskandariya" is, for instance, the land of
the scorpion, a new totem. But it isn't the land or totem she asked
for. Nor is it typical for her to do the asking. And yet, she made the
request, she "asked for a fish", asked not herself or another human—
she asked God:

> but maybe God misheard my request, maybe God thought I said
> not "some sort of fish," but a "scorpion fish," a request he would
> surely have granted, being a goodly God, but then he forgot
> the "fish" attached to the "scorpion" (because God, too, forgets,
> everything forgets)[121]

121. Nytimes.com, https://www.nytimes.com/2005/12/31/opinion/
closing-time-iskandariya.html, accessed December 24, 2024.

I think of Kelly as a land poet, a woodland poet, a poet of dark forests and orchards, cemeteries and gardens, so it's interesting to sense that she may have been seeking the oceanic in the request for fish. Or the river. The lake. The holy body and spirit of water. Instead, she was given the scorpion and the desert, but not necessarily on purpose—perhaps as much by mishearing as by intention—for God holds all means of making on his palette, the making of careful attention, and the making of forgetfulness. An odd characteristic of omniscience. Or is it? If omniscience is all-seeing and all-knowing (and by all-knowing, all-being), wouldn't he also need to know forgetfulness directly, to know it carnally—to forget and have forgotten for himself—not merely to know *of it* like some sentence in book? Indeed—the largest inheres in the smallest: no body without spirit: no existence without being shot through by the presence that pervades all.

Such insistent embodiment is a key trait of Kelly's penetrating intelligence. She didn't leave ideas in the dictionary or in the air. She took them into the blood and, in her poems, gave them flesh and lives to wear. Hence, the fully formed scorpion:

> a peculiar prehistoric creature, part lobster, part spider, part bell-ringer,
> part son of a fallen star, something like a disfigured armored dog, not
> a thing you can eat, or even take on a meaningful walk, so ugly is it,
> so stiffly does it step, as if on ice, freezing again and again in mid-air
> like a listening ear, and then scuttling backwards or leaping madly
> forward, its deadly tail doing a St. Vitus jig. God gave me a scorpion,
> a venomous creature, to be sure, a bug with the bite of Cleopatra's asp,
> but not, as I soon found out, despite the dark gossip, a lover of violence
> or a hater of men.[122]

---

122. Ibid.

"A bug with the bite of Cleopatra's asp"—no random illustration in some an insect-lover's guide book. It's a creature known to her, given to her, studied with the careful attention one pays to a gift. A creature fully admitted into her life, where its character comes into even sharper definition, then ignites a series of similarities:

> In truth, it is shy, the scorpion, a creature with eight eyes and almost no sight, who shuns the daylight, and is driven mad by fire, who favors the lonely spot, and feeds on nothing much, and only throws out its poison barb when backed against a wall—a thing like me[123]

How much work that last phrase does, revealing a litany of personal traits, Kelly's attention having reached a mirror's pitch and polish in the scorpion, then turning back to reflect their shared traits onto herself. "A thing like me," she says. Like her, how? Is she shy? Does she shun a certain kind of light? Does she keep her bite tucked behind her lip unless backed into a wall? Her deep sense of the importance of privacy says *yes*. And the timing of the admission (2005) is curious, given how much attention was piling upon her after publication of *The Orchard* (2004).

What else? What more of her is reflected in this particular insect? Does she have the "eight eyes" of many minds coalesced into her person? Absolutely. And yet, she says, those eyes bear "almost no sight". Given the feverish intensity of her vision, I can't imagine that dim sight is her natural state. What then? Had she worn out her eyes, sapped the facility of vision, or grown estranged from the will to engage it? Had she spent too much time attending to the fiery edges of madness, collecting its visions for our sake,

---

123. Ibid.

but burning her retinas in the process? Whether by spiritual or physical exhaustion, or perhaps a cataract of both, the need for rest, for less light, seems plausible—a rest, if not enforced, at least deeply earned.

But *almost no sight* is not *no sight*, and Kelly could conjure a thousand nights from a crumb. "Iskandariya" traverses new territory in other ways, too. Despite Kelly's shyness and privacy, she invites the scorpion into her home, and invites the poem into her home where it recounts their domestic life together. She becomes "attached," she says, so she cultivates new habits to suit the needs of her armored bell-ringer—she "draw[s] the curtains", "lay[s] out strange dishes", "step[s] softly" and stops speaking, an agreeable arrangement in which she was only stung twice in many years, "both times because, unthinking, I let in the terrible light."[124] This world-shift discloses so much. By letting the scorpion in, and by letting the poem be composed of their relationship, she lets *us* into her private sanctum, revealing yet another layer of her character: kindness.

To shape her life so deeply around the scorpion's needs, to stay her tongue—that magnificent organ of eloquence—and to learn to communicate by gestures of companionship, rather than words, is to show how deeply considerate and caring she was in their bond. The intimate scene divulges direct acts of kindness. A kindness somewhat difficult to discern in her encounters with brutality and death. So often, I could feel a gentle, caring nature at

124. Ibid.

work in the incredible detail of her attentiveness, but rarely was it laid so plain. Again, I'm grateful she gave us that gift.

Of course, the poem could end there but doesn't. The deer is more than deer, and the scorpion is more than scorpion. Towards the end of the poem, as she watches him sleep, she realizes he's a:

> Lung Book or Mortal Book because of his strange organs of breath. His lungs are holes in his body, which open and close. And inside the holes are stiffened membranes, arranged like the pages of a book— imagine that!
> [...]
> He is a house of books, my shy scorpion, carrying in his belly all the perishable manuscripts—a little mirror of the library at Alexandria, which burned.[125]

How prescient the likenesses, which go both ways. He a thing like her, she a thing like him, and his sleeping body providing the means to discover even more of his traits within her. The poet, like the scorpion: a lung book, mortal book, strange organ of breath. The poet: a house of books assembled over a lifetime, over many lifetimes assembled in hers. Kelly: a house of "perishable mansucripts" that cannot stand. Cannot remain. Must dissemble and return. Must burn. The library not perishing, precisely, but needing to be unmade, like the deer, to be remade as someone else, someone emerging from her ashes. An encouraging reason to try to accept the inevitable fire.

After "Iskandariya," it would be four more years before she published the four remaining poems. Another set of fours, another sign? It's a sign if it wants to be, if that's how it presents itself in the mind. What the sign means isn't necessarily material, unless meaning

125. Ibid.

presents itself in turn. My method, generally, is to neither search for hidden meaning nor count on it searching for me. I simply thank the sign and pay attention. For is not the compulsion to pay attention a signal's purpose? Indeed. I pay attention to the timing of the four poems, all of which were published in March and April of 2009. The time of spring, the time of return. Four poems for a four-year hibernation. Given the lengthy nature of the publication process, I'd say there's no way in hell she fully orchestrated the precise timing of their appearance, but she didn't need to: life orchestrated it for her: the poems met their readers in spring: that's how the flowers bloomed.

The timing *is* beautiful, but it presents a problem. A collection of poetry is carefully arranged in a sequence as important as the order of words in a line. The book tells you how to read it, how to journey across its lands. But four poems published across three journals in two months? Not even time can assist me in divining any order Kelly might have assigned to them, but that's okay: there's an order I intuit for my purpose: a series of steps I choose to take to visit the flowers in the garden. One sequence in a series of twenty-four possibilities, each of which has its own validity, but when I look back over Kelly's work, and look ahead to the end of her work, and the end of this book, it's the one that makes the most sense to me.

Here's *my* version, then: "The Wisdom of Solomon," published in the 50th anniversary issue of *The Massachusetts*

Review, in a section called "I Carried the Things I Loved in a Red Sack" (how fitting!), was Kelly's last true lyric, twenty-one lines: ten couplets and an orphan tailender. The poem bloomed in spring and, accordingly, returns us to one of our old, floral friends, the lily, which Kelly trains her eye upon in the night, "the white blades flashing in the room"—the lily, which, like the title, becomes a portal to Solomon, the celebrated king of the Bible, follower of wisdom and divine provenance, poet of flowers and love, and, according to the Quran, a keen communicator with animals.[126]

I begin to think that Solomon may be one of Kelly's archetypes. A suspicion all but confirmed in the biblical "Song of Solomon," also known as the "Song of Songs," the last of the five poetic books in the bible. The Song's second chapter opens, "I am the rose of Sharon, and the lily of the valleys."[127] The rose of Sharon! Kelly's old friend from all the way back in book one, the friend given a poem all its own in book three, one of the familiars Kelly often called into service. Notice, too, the line's multiplicity of self—speaker as human and speaker as rose of Sharon and speaker as lily—a kaleidoscopic selving present throughout much of Kelly's work. The biblical line serves as a model of the portal any creature is: any figment of creation a window into the flow of creativity itself. It's nice to know I can turn to them, the flowers, and them, the biblical lines, to think of what Kelly drew from them. To think

126. Wikipedia.org, https://en.wikipedia.org/wiki/Solomon_in_Islam, accessed December 24, 2024.
127. *The King James Version Standard Bible*, https://www.kingjamesbibleonline.org/Song-of-Solomon-2-1/, accessed December 24, 2024.

of what might still be drawn.

I think there's another turn in Kelly at play here. The biblical "Song of Solomon" is a book of love—romantic love, a love of nature, and divine love—a book of poetry that teaches, one might say, "bliss through union."[128] I think Kelly is seeking in her last poems, however consciously, to meditate upon some union, to find her way from the lilies to Solomon and back to the lilies with new eyes: to see that they are no longer just lilies: they are also "the body of god."[129] In a grander sense, she's learning to see not only the multiplicity of self, which she excels at, but the singularity that expresses itself through the multiplicity. It's no easy path to think oneself along. It's vulnerable, and feels important that she's letting down her guard again, inviting us into the room and into her mind, which spins, "thinking of the lilies," and:

> of Solomon, and his robes, and his crowns,
> the hands that wove, and the hands that hammered,
>
> the words tossed to pass the time, and the river
> of dark song that rows the day[130]

The encounters along the path are just as important as the summit of union. They are, ultimately, expressions of the unity already present. And acknowledgment of the encounters is a gesture of gratitude for their company and their assistance: the more acknowledgment, the more gratitude: not just for the fruit, but

128. J. Sidlow Baxter, *Explore the Book*, "The Poetical Books," Zondervan (1966), 13.
129. Brigit Pegeen Kelly, "The Wisdom of Solomon," *The Massachusetts Review*, Vol. 50, No. 1/2 (Spring/Summer 2009), 231.
130. Ibid.

for the long-ripening branches that yield it. Gratitude for the robes and crowns—beautiful, gaudy ephemera—yes, but also for the hands that wove and hammered, the hands that ached and crafted with care, crafted in fear of getting something wrong and being disfigured, hands that were sore and needed someone to rub them at night. Hands that worked with pride and hands that hurt, at boring, laborious work, so the heads connected to the hands tossed words at one another to soften the rough handling of time, to preoccupy the part of themselves that wanted to quit. But there's no quitting on divine time. Divine journeys are unceasing. Being is always on. The song of being is always being sung: "the river / of dark song that rows the day." It rows the day, it rows the night. It rows Kelly. Rows the lilies. Rows the rose of Sharon and Solomon and his wisdom. Rows the lover who rubs her beloved's aching hands, and the muscles that soften in gratitude when the ache of living leaves them.

Still, the path calls, so Kelly forges ahead. A continuous thinking becomes another kind of ache: "thinking in the night, / when thought is not itself, but a phantom creature— // half plucked bird, half torn man, unable / to call up its name".[131] The mind itself is the phantom creature, the deer portal, the animal it's about to become not yet assuming its form, or perhaps the phantom is exhausted of forms, of forming, unable to recall even its own name. The dark song rows, then, the poet out to the edge of poetry, to the edge of making, to the edge of selving, towards that which

---

131. Ibid.

all singing—verbal, biological, universal—becomes. The singing surrenders to song, the inexhaustible hum, which continues to propel the singers who haven't yet exhausted their voices:

> [...] Oh, think of them, the lilies,
>
> all naked in the pasture, all undismayed by
> any high notion of themselves, and think
>
> of poor Solomon, in all his glory, who had not
> the sure wit of one small flower, nor could he
>
> in his encrusted robes mirror—as each lily does—
> the body of god lying on the waters,
>
> the unclothed body of god.[132]

Here again Kelly hearkens to the bible, to the Gospel of Luke, 12:27, part of the "do not worry" passage (12:22-12:34), wherein Jesus counsels against anxiety, counsels faith in divine providence, and faith in the divinity immanent (yet imbued with transcendent grace) in the lily:

> Consider the lilies, how they grow: they toil not,
> they spin not; and yet I say unto you, that Solomon
> in all his glory was not arrayed like one of these.[133]

The lilies are, as Kelly put it, "undismayed by / any high notion of themselves", and have—by nature, not by achievement or status— more wit, splendor and glory than even Solomon at the height of his wealth and wisdom. The gospel reminds us that the gift of being is a glory surpassing any riches that might issue from our desires and deeds. A gift of glory: the dark river of song that rows us, in

---

132. Ibid.
133. *The King James Version Standard Bible,* https://www.kingjamesbibleonline.org/Luke-12-27/, accessed December 24, 2024.

body and out: in the lily in the valley, and in the body the lily abides

in: "the body of god lying on the waters, / the unclothed body of

god."[134] Throughout and beyond her forms and names, Kelly's being

and body is continuous with the lily's, shares its providence and

grace—Kelly abides in god's body, too. Abides *in*, and abides *as*: our

movements the movements of divinity, embodied in every sense

and act. God: the dark river of song that rows the blood and the sap

alike: our lives the myriad flowers blooming on the rose of Sharon.

If "Iskandariya" and "The Wisdom of Solomon" were

departures in terms of letting us into her domestic life and spiritual

meditations, I would say that her next two works, "Geisblatt"

and "A Curious Cologne," are equal departures in terms of style,

atmosphere and focus. Published in the April 2009 issue of *The Yale

Review*, they took the conversational prose style of "Iskandariya"

and turned it up at least a half dozen notches. From one perspective,

they seem as much like a poet's trip reports or letters from abroad

as they do "poems," although I believe that at a certain point for

certain poets, all writing becomes poetry, just in different forms:

poetry in the form of verse, poetry in the form of a letter, poetry

in the form of a novel. And for a subset of those, all movement

becomes poetry: poetry in the form of life and existence itself, a

poem in which we participate as it writes us, brief currents in the

river of song.

But for now, we're still in the garden, walking from poem

---

134. Brigit Pegeen Kelly, "The Wisdom of Solomon," *The Massachu-setts Review*, Vol. 50, No. 1/2 (Spring/Summer 2009), 231.

to poem, from lilies to *geißblatt*, German for honeysuckle, another floral friend who's been with us since *Trumpets*. It's comforting to know that Kelly stuck by her friends. A friend who has been, and still contains, many versions of the self we share. At first, "Geisblatt" feels like the recollection of a vision:

> The sun came up, the birds whistled, the honeysuckle bloomed— [...] with such unbounded fervor it obliterated the far-off cries... but maybe we should have paid heed to how the swarming gold brought on a kind of delirium, as if the gold were not innumerable blooms commingling, but clouds of those long-legged needling insects, which are, it is true, indescribably beautiful, but deadly nonetheless, and more deadly en masse, inducing a kind of sleeping sickness, a kind of wasting sickness that renders one incapable of rising from bed, or rising clearly into a single thought...[135]

And it *is* a vision recounted, but it's also something else, something less sober, more delirious: I think we're entering the honeysuckle itself, entering the land that exists within the body of the flower, as we exist within the body of Earth. That's one possible story, or version of a story that traverses several planes. Perhaps, alternatively or in addition, the sight of honeysuckle in full bloom was enough to induce delirium on *this* plane, the sweet smell a further induction, the mounting delirium opening the portal into honeysuckle's interior realm. The delirium which *should, maybe,* have been a warning against entrance, the sign of a sickening entrancement rather than an entrancement of kindly wonder, a sickening that fractures thought and in so doing leaves one open to possession through the cracks: "the honeysuckle being, as it were, a / creature of multiple natures, as if possessed by many demons, /

135. Brigit Pegeen Kelly, "Geisblatt," *The Yale Review*, Volume 97, Issue 2 (April 2009), 18.

sometimes mounding, sometimes swooning, sometimes thrusting / its arms straight up". From the scorpion God to the god of the lily to the soul's possession by a pack of demons, it seems that Kelly's focus on the spiritual realm deepens in these final poems. Which isn't to say that she hadn't taken us there before, but that we may be squarely planted there straight through until the end. Indeed, there's not one mention of the heart in these last poems, as though Kelly were training her gaze on the parts of herself that might survive her body and mind.

In *this* poem, however, Kelly continues reckoning with possession. If she sees in the lily the body of god, and if she sees in the honeysuckle a pack of demons, and if the pack of demons is likewise constituted by the body of god, does it not follow that god possesses in both holy and unholy ways? Holy, yes:

> the single blossom is a stringy affair, a piece of pronged
> flesh, of ruinous color, fermented yellow, and inverted
> like a divining rod, pointing straight down, yes,
> a beneficent instrument nailing the exact watery spot[136]

In one version of itself, possessed by its better demons, the honeysuckle acts as a divine instrument, alerting the thirsty to the water beneath the bush, the holy water our bodies so direly need. But there is also warning in its tissue, an evident warning "of ruinous color, fermented yellow," as though it were rotting from within. Is that a bad sign? All living creatures must rot. It's a function of the way the dark river carries song from body to body, voice to voice, needing bodies to degenerate and regenerate into other bodies so

---

136. Ibid.

the process of embodied singing has a means to continue. But no nature is simply good. Nor simply bad. Always complexly both (and neither) in innate, singular union. Holy, yes, and unholy, too, for the honesuckle is also:

> less like that, like a tool of divination, than like a man
> forcibly turned upside down, his arms splayed, as Peter's
> arms were splayed, his feet bound, the bush snagged
> all over with little Peters, a bush of shrunken martyrs,
> a gaseous lit ball turning in the air like a Catherine Wheel,
> a thing I have never seen, and therefore should not speak of,
> some gold confounding horror or blessing, made now,
> in this time, this fateful place, into no more than a party favor,
> a tree of poppets, the crowning curiosity of some flamboyant
> festival, designed—while the city burns—to distract the king.[137]

So much to unpack in this convergence of realms. Beneath the honeysuckle of the divining rod, Kelly discovers the honeysuckle of Peter's crucifixion, landing us back in early Christian lore. Peter met his end while preaching in Rome, following the Great Fire of Rome in 64 AD. Some accused the king, Nero, of setting the fire to clear space for his building projects,[138] while Nero deflected and accused the Christians, embarking on a vicious persecution against leaders and members of the faith.[139] Peter, the apostle—a prime scapegoat—was sentenced to death by crucifixion, the sentence given to non-Romans—Paul, meanwhile, was given the Roman sentence of beheading.[140] At his crucifixion, Peter asked to be crucified upside down, in part out of deference to his Lord, and in part because he

---

137. Ibid.
138. Wikipedia.org, https://en.wikipedia.org/wiki/Nero, accessed December 30, 2024.
139. Wikipedia.org, https://en.wikipedia.org/wiki/Great_Fire_of_Rome, accessed December 30, 2024.
140. Jacobus de Voragine, *The Golden Legend: Readings on the Saints*, "89. Saint Peter, Apostle," Princeton University Press (2012), 345.

believed that his Lord would call him from Earth to Heaven, and therefore had to enter divinity by relinquishing his soul to the soul of Earth.[141] Surrendering his presence in the dark song to hers, Mother Earth in turn eventually surrendering to the Heavenly presences that comprise her. Peter returned to Earth and Nero died by suicide a few years later.[142] The song sings us into being and the song sings us out. Rome rose and Rome fell. Christianity continued to grow.

How did Kelly discern Peter's upside-down crucifixion in the honeysuckle? In the manner of its singing: one petal facing downward (the head), and several petals facing up (the legs). Head down: also the gesture of prayer. The honeysuckle multiplied: divining rod, Rome, crucifixion, martyr, a whole "bush of shrunken martyrs"—holy—which turn into a Catherine Wheel—unholy—a medieval torture device used to break bones and maim, then to behead, if lucky, or left to die on the vine in slow agony, if not. Kelly lays witness to both blessing and horror, grace and torture—grave, serious matters to which humans grow sickeningly accustomed and unbothered—and then she ends the poem with a resigned yet defiant lament: the splendor now "no more than a party favor," a "crowning curiosity of some flamboyant festival," but not without its dark side, for the splendor is "designed—while the city burns— to distract the king."[143]

141. Ibid., 345-346.
142. Wikipedia.org, https://en.wikipedia.org/wiki/Nero, accessed December 30, 2024.
143. Brigit Pegeen Kelly, "Geisblatt," *The Yale Review*, Volume 97, Issue 2 (April 2009), 18.

What to make of this ending in the context of the last poems? Again, we're dealing with spiritual matters, complicating the recognition of the body of god in the lily, with the recognition in the honeysuckle that the body grips us with both holy and unholy possession. I think there's more to it: a subtle, double-sided parable taking shape. A warning against the dangers of easy infatuation on the one hand, and against smug indifference on the other. If we're too easily infatuated or beguiled, we may fall prey to the deliriums of pleasure, which may slowly become vice and disentangle the threads of our sanity. Or worse, we may be like the king, caught up in baubles while the city burns. Or the drunk, fingering the bottle, while his liver drowns.

Conversely, if we become apathetic to the sheer force and grace at work in every experience and creature, we may wallow like half-dead phantoms in the shallows of indifference, our faculties of attention and passion deteriorating in our souls, devolving until we see nothing of the countless realms in the flower, not even beauty— just a thing, another lesser, stupid thing to be ignored. Kelly is countenancing us to pay attention, to value the divine splendor in our faculties, and to cultivate our faculties that we might more deeply experience the riches of Earthly existence. But she's also countenancing us to be careful about the kinds and degrees of attention we pay, the hazards of delirium, addiction and madness that might sneak up on us from behind, or right under our nose. And to be discerning of the kinds and purposes of attention paid to us, both from our plane and from the planes intersecting with ours. In a world of witness, most of the witness is happening in species other than human. Humans who ignore or remain indifferent to the wonders, dangers and burning of the world to our peril.

To be grateful but careful: an ethic for a life well lived.

The other *Yale* poem, "A Curious Cologne," bests its priors in terms of pure departureship by a mile. A rather breezy epistolary, so clearly cast in modern times with modern adornments, I could never have guessed it issued from Kelly's pen. Placing us in modernity isn't a bad thing, but it's surprising—in truth, I'm not sure how I feel about that aspect of the poem—but breezy for Kelly is still rather heavy for us mortals: a trip to a museum with a museum director, under Kelly's gaze: by now, we can imagine what she might see. Or can we?

The poem opens with a little letting in: "How bad my handwriting is."[144] For a doctor, this makes little difference, but for a poet, whose every word may alter worlds: what if she can't read her own writing? What might be lost in the scribble? The museum director's name, for one:

> [...] I copied down the Museum Director's name, and when
> I went back to read it I thought it said Bullrecks, clearly
> the wrong name, but quite a comic name for a Museum Director,
> bringing to mind, as it does, a bull in a china shop, though
> the exhibit in question, the one the Director was commenting
> upon, was not of Chinese Glass, or Minoan Pottery, but of
> pictures of Jesus. "Antique pictures," to be exact, though
> the announcement in the paper said only "pictures of Jesus."[145]

---

144. Ibid., "A Curious Cologne," 19-20.
145. Ibid.

God, Peter, Jesus: clearly the Christian world of her Catholic faith is on her mind, but at this stage of life, the order and import of that world doesn't feel like the trappings of fixed tradition. The faith and its figures, like the statues, like the flowers, like the deer, dynamically shift and turn and evolve. Kelly isn't a child being forced to go to church and suffer its stuffy interpretation of the world, she's turning towards its realm as the interpreter, with the full force of her hyper-attentive, blessing-and-horror-wise eye. The kind of eye that sees more than mere scribble and error in the indecipherable director's name: she sees a bull, a China shop, Chinese Glass, Minoan pottery, a wealth of being with plenty more to see until she looks away.

She looks, now, towards Jesus, or two versions of Jesus, and the considerable difference cast by a single qualifier—antique:

> How different those two things are, "pictures" and "antique pictures." The antique Jesus is grave, and lily white, or lead yellow, draped like a dead swan backwards over his mother's knee, or lost in shrouded thought, or bleeding like a rose among the rocks, while the new Jesus, on the pamphlets brought to your door, or on the billboards, the same Jesus reproduced with slight variation a million times over on cards and books and shirts, is a Jesus so pastel he would melt in a minor rain.[146]

The first half of the second sentence streams like a parade of Kellyean characters: the lily, white shifting to yellow, the dead swan, shrouded thought, a bleeding rose. If these are symbols of the antique, then Kelly is assuredly a member of the antique congregation. To even mention the sterilized, whitewashed version of life would be to time-travel radically forward in most of

146. Ibid.

her poems. To arrive in a land of mass reproduction and kitschery, rather than mysterious creatures and hand-carved statues: pamphlets, billboards, cards and books and shirts: a watering down of life's concentrated essence—just look what it did to Jesus: a man become so slight and "so pastel he would melt in a minor rain." Whew: the heat coming off that final blazing line makes me pull my face back from the fire.

It's a symptom of something sad, gone wrong, the worth of phenomena and our own creativity undervalued. A common artistic bravery that gets relegated to daring souls we mock as deranged actors with disfigured minds, practically insane:

> People, it seems have given up on making solemn pictures of Jesus—except, of course, for the band of brave artists devoted to disfiguring Jesus. They dip Jesus in urine, or smear pig's blood in Jesus's curly hair, or bind Jesus in hundreds of colored chains and whips, and sometimes we go to look at these Jesuses, and we think about lunch, or the peculiar unstable weather, or the sad man on the museum steps waving a warning placard back and forth slowly like a sail without a ship...[147]

And yet even their outrageous maneuvers meant to stimulate our feelings fall flat. Their flirtations with madness might as well be the grey sky to us who think we have seen so much, we swindle ourselves into seeing little, feeling less, the deficiency in attentiveness blinding us to the diminishment of experience. Kelly's stepping all the way into the present to better admonish this half-life flipped on cruise control, lamenting how much we lose when the fourteen-billion-year act of creativity in which we participate is regarded as the drudgery of another tossable day.

147. Ibid.

So, Kelly turns towards her own museum adventure, leading by example, accompanied by "Director Bluehm", "a very sober name, a proper name" for "a proper man, not like his friend Mr. Bullrecks at all." Note the relationship between these two versions of himself is one of friendship, rather than the antithetical relationship of a Jekyll and Hyde—a comforting thought. Director Bluehm, orienting Kelly to the current state of the exhibit:

> was commenting on the latest addition to the "exhibit of antique Jesuses," a "guest exhibit," as the graceful man who took off his clothes and climbed onto a table and stood perfectly still beside a picture of "The Crucified Lord" described himself, a "guest exhibit," a ghostly display, which was lowered quickly and taken away by men in blue suits. And "regrettable" was the way the Museum Director described the "uninvited exhibit," regrettable but not fatal, since none of the "real artworks were destroyed."[148]

In quoting choice phrases, Kelly directs our attention. The director found the naked exhibit "regrettable," but not regrettable enough to keep it quiet: he had a little tipple to share. Ah, he *had* felt something. It's rather remarkable, actually. The exhibit of *antique* Jesuses steps like Kelly into the present, admitting a guest exhibitor, the scripture of his living flesh being hosted by the Jesuses on the wall, and by the divinity in the room. Of course, the men who abide by faith in human law, not by divine splendor, ensure he is "lowered quickly and taken away", "uninvited" as he was by their bosses and senses of propriety, lest his lesser flesh tarnish the "real artworks" with the less real artistry of his body and soul. Director Bleuhm seems rather oblivious to the diminishment of his vision, the distortions of his language, and the pomposity of his judgment.

148. Ibid.

The director being a living symbol of a widespread, societal ill.

Let's say, for argument's sake, that the exhibitionist was intoxicated. Even so, his act was neither violent nor a hindrance to what may transpire between soul and art in the hosting space of a museum. He merely "took off his / clothes and climbed onto a table and stood perfectly still", a "graceful" act amidst an exhibit of grace's incarnation, an exhibit of the divine creativity at work in the artistry of his life and his living form, and more than that: the artistry of life itself: the dark river of song that sings us all. Had the man entered an ancient tavern, had a few, listened to Jesus praise holy providence in every creature from atop a table, then decided to climb up beside Jesus, disrobe and quietly pose, I highly doubt Jesus would have minded. He might even have regarded the act as the living manifestation of his teaching, a heightening of the divine presence in the room, and an electrification of the presences attending to its works.

Indeed, how much the room would shift, even after the man left or, in our time, was taken away. The "real artworks" having been heightened by his creative contributions, certainly not diminished, harmed or, heaven perish the thought—*destroyed*:

> Indeed not. Indeed not. For how electrified those somber pictures seemed to be in the hush following the great stir, how radiant the light shining on the vast blue distances, and the carved and gilded frames, and all the brooding Jesuses, everything humming together like a neon installation celebrating the whole absurd affair.[149]

If "Geisblatt" offers a subtle parable, "A Curious Cologne" ascends

---

149. Ibid.

the lectern to belt its reverential teaching loud and clear. Art—
the art we love and laud, the art we profess to live for and hold
dear—isn't just painted on the canvas within the gilded frames
upon the wall. It isn't just the thousands of hours rent from heart
and flesh to carve statues that bore or mesmerize as we wander
rainy cemeteries and gardens. It's the naked man who crawls up
beside an antique painting of Jesus, suturing the two worlds. It's
the air that stirs when he is snatched and sent on his deflated way.
It's the "radiant light shining on the vast blue distances", and the
trees that once swayed in the sky and hosted birds and sheltered
deer, then sacrificed their arboreal lives to frame the face of Jesus.
Art is the ghosts whose bodies form the pages upon which these
thoughts and feelings find a worldly home. It's my affection for
Kelly's work and my hope for the pleasure readers may encounter
in this expression of warmth. It's me, you, us, and the thing which
isn't a thing but a being we are before, during and after our brief
sojourn as human.

As Kelly reminds us, art is creativity incarnate, whether
in the museum or in the past or in the extinct species whose tales
are recorded in the rock, the species who are the rock itself, and
are the ancestral bodies that grant us the facilities of attention and
admiration. Where something is, where we are, we are *of* art, and
we *are art itself.* Participating in its creations and destructions and
transformations. The painter is an artist. Kelly is an artist. The
carpenter and the bee. The paint and pen, how and why, where and

when. I'll say it again: *art is creativity incarnate*. Even breath—yes—lowly, holy breathing is an innately artistic act. As is longing, as is regret, as is madness, as is love. It's "everything humming together like a neon installation celebrating the whole absurd affair." To be is to be art, the art of the Earth, the art of the Universe, and the art of what can't be said. To be is to be the dark river of song, its currents and its rapids and the very movement of its flow.

No part not participant, each part both comprising and belonging to the whole.

These are not Kelly's thoughts, nor are they precisely mine, they're what I am able to witness, the vision I am blessed to cultivate and communicate under the spell of Kelly's influence, and under the spell of love a poet has for the guides who most deeply shape his sense of language and his sense of the poetic soul. All of us are soulful influences at work in the traditions of art—be it walks in the woods or useful handiwork or a symphony in Central Park—and all of us are influentially at work in one another, literally becoming the others we touch, and they us. Think how many influences there are in the Kelly, known and unknown, and in her mentors and theirs and so on, and in the personal constellation of *my* masters—Kelly, Berry, Graham, Harjo, Wilner, Hugo, Rumi and Rilke—the last of which I share with Kelly, through him and through her and through the countless others who drank from Rainer's song and found themselves transformed.

Think of how many influences there are in any

phenomenon or creature—the animals, plants, minerals and elements; the lifeforms and landscapes; the stars spent and ancestors dead, but still residing. Think of the 99% of all species who ever lived, then went extinct, but in so doing they gave rise to the ones we know and love—they give rise to ourselves in this enormous and heartbreaking ancestry. Kelly pushes us to pay attention, such careful, nuanced attention, as if our lives depended on it, as if both the quality and continuity of life itself was at stake. She fervently attends to the many layers and realms in each deer and curve of stone, each lily and naked man, to learn their worth, I think, and to fuel her gratitude, each layer her vision reaches revealing another blessing to be thankful for, each rise in the capacity of vision enabling a rise in the capacity of appreciation, enabling Kelly (and us) to work endlessly towards the divine state of *unlimited gratitude*.

To what end? For art's sake? For gratitude's sake? For her soul's sake? For her family? Yes, but not only that. To me, it's for a larger sake, a critical, life-loving and life-saving purpose. If attentiveness breeds familiarity, and if familiarity breeds gratitude, what effect does such gratitude have on our lives, our behavior, the world? Think of the destructiveness wrought by a mere century's worth of anthropocentrism and greed, the kinds of tunnel vision contracted by imagining ourselves as centers of importance, seeking unlimited material wealth. The sense of entitlement over providence, the sense of ownership over belonging, the sense of individuality over mutuality: our shared welfare and future: shared life, shared health, shared wealth, shared planet, shared being, shared song, shared soul.

It's a radical question of orientation. Are Mother Earth and our lives and life itself gifts to cherish and take care of, or taken-for-granted resources to subdue and exhaust in service of shortsighted and personal desires? Are the landscapes and creatures that enliven us ours, or are we theirs, or do we belong to one another in a collective compulsion to continue? Not continue individually at the expense of one another, but continue collectively in furtherance of life itself. Life—biology—is a process, a species-manifesting and species-extinguishing process, and we're parts of the process, notes in the song, responsible to the integrity of the music, upon which depends the welfare of all species and specimens. Simply put, either we learn to live on the terms by which the process flourishes, or we degrade the process until it can no longer sustain us and we disappear. Now I'm preaching alongside Kelly, but bear with me a smidge longer.

The process, the music, moves through us—good and ill, dissonant and harmonic—moves in ways we can never detect or fathom, let alone comprehend. Say we're a denouement. Say we're too far gone and consume ourselves into oblivion. It's sad to be our own agents of doom, but we're not the first species or geophysical force to wreak planetary havoc and swing extinction's scythe. Say, furthermore, that our clearing of the stage allows a new version of life to emerge. Say we're the end of a verse, initiating the next, the new species of the new verse equally deserving of their time within the song. We've seen this cycle repeated in the book of rock beneath us. It has come to pass and shall again.

But we don't know that we're a denouement.

We could be a climax and a crash on the way to a lull. And we're not the only ones living in the song. A million other *species* stand to be slaughtered by our attempt to make the music not a music of lively flourishing and gratitude and care, but a music about a self-serving species and its attempt to dominate forces of which it is a speck. For shame. But the music's still alive in us and this is where I think Kelly's work may lead us: if attentiveness exposes us to the immense depth and wealth of providence, and if it cultivates in us a gratitude both for divinity's gifts and for its manner of providing, and if that gift is understood to be a common good, a gift inhabited and shared, then it seems only natural that we might begin to shift towards an ethic of care—to receive the gift, admire it and endeavor to care for its continuance, given as it was in Motherly, Earthly love, given as it will be from us to those who follow. Do we want to give a gift broken, neglected and abused? I think not. It's all overwhelming, to be sure, and it's good to keep in mind that one can only do one's small part—or outsized part in Kelly's case—then pray. For my part, I find that Kelly's keen sense of care and gratitude are contagious, and they make me want to be a better caretaker of our gifts.

Okay, enough from me; thank you for listening; I'll step down from the lectern.

Back on the ground, I turn towards Kelly's last poem, or the last I know, and on the one hand, I'm relieved to see a spot of rest for myself ahead, but on the other, I mourn there being no new Kelly poems to send me exploring and admiring on my way to praise. The mourning lasts a moment, two, six, then I remember all the paths yet untaken through her work, that there are more paths than I can ever find, let alone explore—I'll exhaust myself, but never them. Hence the mourning shifts again to gratitude for the richness and the world-multiplying portals still in store. I head to the bathroom, look out the window and there she is: I wave to the grazing deer.

Kelly's last poem returns us to Peter's resting place: "Rome," published in the spring issue of *Ploughshares*, 2009. I just pulled up the cover of that issue and cracked a buoyant smile: it was guest edited by Eleanor Wilner, one of my holy influences, with whom I've had a sparse but kind and encouraging correspondence. I'm smiling for another reason, too. One day, I sent Eleanor a fan letter and eight poems in gratitude, as poets do. She didn't know me from Adam, but she graciously responded to the work, noting that "you have a wonderfully protean imagination, one thing turning into another, everything loaning life and motion to the next".[150] As it happens in synchronicities, a few days ago that line popped into my head while I was walking and thinking of this

150. Eleanor Wilner, Private Correspondence (2018).

essay. It came to me as a perfect description not of my work, but of Kelly's, and it dawns on me now: *of course, I get that from her, it's one of Kelly's (and Wilner's) marks on me.* Thank you for that realization, Eleanor, and thank you, Brigit.

And thank *you*: dark river of song.

Different as the last poems may be—there are several departures in style and content between them and prior works, and between one another—there are also continuities. The god of relationship in Iskandariya and the scorpion. The body of god within Solomon and the providential lily. The god of delirium and death in the honeysuckle and Peter's Rome. The god of art and the living body, naked beside the picture of Jesus. All of them a letting in. A sharing *of*, and a sharing *with*. It feels as though it wasn't me who chose the path through these final flowers in Kelly's garden. It feels as though I have been given a vision and ushered between the poems in a pattern that traces the connections between all that Kelly felt and spoke. It feels as though I have gone out on a journey, and am going home now, with one last stop to make.

It is only fitting, then, that we return to Rome and roses, to statuary and the totem of the wild creature, to Kelly the storyteller-oracle, to a poem so tightly woven and lucidly spoken it lands me squarely back in my favorite land of hers, *The Orchard.* "Rome" is cut from the Kelly of old, the antique Kelly, Kelly at her best, as Amy Gerstler agreed, choosing it from among Kelly's 2009 quartet for inclusion in the following year's *Best American Poetry.*

In Gerstler's introduction, she says, "in ancient Mesopotamia, a culture perhaps not so different from our own, there were five basic job descriptions for poets:

1. Astrologer/scribe
2. Diviner
3. Exorcist/magician
4. Physician
5. Lamentation chanter"[151]

I immediately recognize four of these in Kelly, five depending on how the medicine goes down. Gerstler says she'd choose the last job for herself, then muses that "we read and compose poems to soothe our babies, to chat up the gods, to remember what happened yesterday and back in 2,500 BCE, and to muse about what changes and never will."[152] Surely Kelly's spirit circles back and forth in the latter half of that sentence. Gerstler also says, "lose touch with wonderment and you're fucked."[153] Ha! That's Kelly to a tee: keeping the blessing-horror of wonderment alive.

I'm procrastinating, committing sins of tangency, circling the last poem too many times without meeting it head on, I know. I'm sure you can guess why. A page later, I'll have to let go, and I don't want to, want to linger as long as I can. Forgive me this dallying. But it's also because I'm discovering new sides of Kelly in the words of Wilner and Gerstler, sides that I intuited but couldn't articulate, and sides I hadn't noticed until I found myself looking through their many-minded eyes. More sight, more capacity for gratitude:

151. Amy Gerstler, Ed., *The Best American Poetry 2010,* "Introduction by Amy Gerstler," Scribner (2010), xxii.
152. Ibid., xxiii.
153. Ibid., xxi.

their insights enable me to go into Kelly's last poem, I hope, with sharper senses than I would have without them standing on my shoulders, whispering in my ears.

Here's "Rome," then, in full:

Rome

I saw once, in a rose garden, a remarkable statue of the Roman she-wolf and her twins, a reproduction of an ancient statue—not the famous bronze statue, so often copied, in which the wolf's blunt head swings forward toward the viewer like a sad battering ram, but an even older statue, of provenance less clear. The wolf had been cut out of black stone, made blacker by the garden's shadows, and she stood in profile, her elegant head pointed toward something far beyond her, her long unmarked body and legs—narrower and more finely-boned than the body and legs of wolves as we know them—possessed, it seemed, of a great stillness, like the saturated stillness of the roses, but tightly-nerved, set, on the instant, to move. Under her belly, stood the boys, under her black breasts, not babes, as one might expect, but two lean boys, cut from the same shadowed stone as the wolf, but disproportionately small, grown boys no bigger than starlings, though still, like the wolf, oddly fine of face and limb, one boy pressing four fingers against one long breast, his other hand cupped beneath it to catch the falling milk, the second boy wrapping both arms around another breast, as if to carry it off, neither boy suckling, both instead turned toward you, dreamy, sweetly sly, as if to chide you for interrupting their feeding, or as if they were plotting a good trick... Beautiful, those boys among the roses. Beautiful, the black wolf. But it was the breasts that held the eye, a double row of four black breasts, eight smooth breasts, each narrowing to a strict point, piercing sharp, exactly the shape of the ivory tooth of the shark.[154]

I'm quoting the poem in full because I couldn't find a natural breaking point at which to interject, which I think tells me the poem wants to be considered as a whole. A statue still intact, however worn or broken its parts. A singular thriving. By "wants"

154. Brigit Pegeen Kelly, "Rome," *Ploughshares*, Vol. 35, No. 1 (Spring 2009), 104.

I don't mean it has biological desires (but it might). I mean its tendency to elicit a response takes a certain shape—it draws me towards a certain mode of contemplation. The kind of desire a seed has for a flower. The kind of desire milk has for life. I'm also quoting it in full because I find myself rather struck through with quietude, the ideas and interpretations still forming—a quietude that's part awe, part reverence, part reeling curiosity that roves up and down the lines, trying to understand the particular magic that just transpired.

It was a mixture of several things. At the point when Kelly conjures the boys beneath the she-wolf's belly, a shudder of déjà vu passed through me like a ghost. I know this place; I've been here before; it's etched in me already, and the person I was at that time is coming to say hello. I know this poem because a part of its effect is unforgettable. The wolf, my own totem figure, mothering boys with her milk, while her body is lean, tense, poised as if for a fight, perhaps protecting her boys, perhaps readying herself to confront the unknown danger she senses heading towards her, a stance from which to protect her soul, and all she cares about, and all she carries within her.

I remembered, then: I'd read the anthology long ago in New York City, after a day at Poets House on Spring Street, enjoying libations at my favorite tavern, d.b.a. It was dusk or dark and I was sitting at a table looking out on the street, and from the world of modern poetry this eerie, arresting realm from god knows when and where had emerged, marking me and altering the atmosphere around me. I should say that I have aphantasia and a terrible memory for names, could never have told you who wrote the poem or what book it was in, but feelings and atmospheres stick with me, and that night grips me still. How fitting: the last poem is an old acquaintance, the distance of time and a shared moment making it feel like a friend.

I'm grateful for the chance to meet the poem again, to get to know it much better. To that end, I'd like this analysis to meet Kelly in both worlds: the realm of the poem and the realm of the statue. I have spent the last few days trying to find a picture of the statue without luck. Neither my Google skills nor Chat GPT could find her, although I think I found a version of her, or at least a close relative. So let's go back even further. Who is this she-wolf? Who are the boys? What in tarnation is going on?

I don't generally care for the need to fill in backstory or research allusions in a poem, and I truly don't think it's necessary or particularly enriching for the poems in Kelly's books, but these last poems move in a different manner. To me, they move from and across Kelly's inner world, her subconscious world—they include and subsume her vision—and they carry a personal history and story not altogether missing from her prior work, but certainly held back in the shadows. Even this scene, so cut from the cloth of *The Orchard*, depends on her personal encounter with a unique rendition of a well-known work. We're in her memory, as if at the end of things, looking back at the one point of creation that draws her attention out of all she found and made. For this, and for Kelly, I seek out the history, the hidden story, that I might more deeply share the experience of the memory as it moves her.

The she-wolf is Luperca, often simply known as Lupa, without whom there would be no Rome.[155] The boys, it turns out, are not hers, at least not of her womb, though they shall always carry her lifeforce, having been saved from death by her milk.[156] The story starts with them, and with their biological mother, Rhea Siliva, a descendant of Aeneas who, when her father king Numitor of Alba Longa was usurped by his brother Amulius, was forced to become a Vestal Virgin, a priestess of the goddess Vesta,[157] priestesses selected as children to serve terms of thirty years.[158]

The priestesses were sworn to celibacy and held in extremely high regard. The later Roman Vestals were given sovereignty over themselves, answerable only to Rome's highest priest.[159] They were considered sacrosanct, a physical embodiment of Rome and its gods, free to perform acts in violation of Roman law, such as writing their own wills and granting property to women.[160] But when Rhea was a priestess of Alba Longa, Rome was not yet

155. T.P. Wiseman, "The God of the Lupercal," *Journal of Roman Studies, Vol. 85* (1995), 1.
156. Wikipedia.org, https://en.wikipedia.org/wiki/She-wolf_(Roman_mythology), accessed December 30, 2024.
157. Wikipedia.org, https://en.wikipedia.org/wiki/Rhea_Silvia, accessed December 30, 2024.
158. Wikipedia.org, https://en.wikipedia.org/wiki/Vestal_Virgin, accessed December 30, 2024.
159. Ibid.
160. Ibid.

born, was literally a phantom future in her womb. A future born of violence, for when, one day, Rhea went to a sacred grove of the god Mars to get water for the temple, Mars raped her, impregnating her with the twins Romulus and Remus.[161] Or, according to another version, she was raped by an unknown man and, to try to save herself, claimed the children were of divine conception.[162]

Typically, she'd be buried alive, but Amulius feared the wrath of a paternal god, so he imprisoned Rhea and ordered the twins to be murdered by a servant. The servant, instead, took pity on the babes, and sent them down the river Tiber in a basket. The river god Tibernius stepped in as an agent of grace, too, calming the waters and placing the basket in the roots of a fig tree in Lupercal, a cave situated at the heart of future Rome.[163] There the she-wolf found them and suckled them, saving them from death. The twins grew up tending flocks, unaware of their identities. Eventually they learned who they were and took revenge on their granduncle, restoring their grandfather as king. They then agreed to found a city in their farmland, but in an argument over the proper cite, Remus was killed by Romulus or one of his followers.[164] Hence Rome rose to greatness and Reme never came to be. The heart of the Empire and future Italy survived millennia, and Luperca became one of Rome's mothers, Rhea the people's mother from the human realm,

161. Wikipedia.org, https://en.wikipedia.org/wiki/Rhea_Silvia, accessed December 30, 2024.
162. Worldhistory.org, https://www.worldhistory.org/Romulus_and_Remus/, accessed December 30, 2024.
163. Ibid.
164. Wikipedia.org, https://en.wikipedia.org/wiki/Romulus_and_Remus, accessed December 30, 2024.

Luperca their wild mother from the woods.

Now the road leads us back to Kelly's "Rome," with greater appreciation for this holy wolf, who became many wolves and mother figure to many people. But for now, it's the wolf of Kelly's memory who shepherds us through the end of her work. Notice Kelly's attention to the position of Luperca's head, neither swung "toward the viewer" like the famous Capitoline statue; nor eyeing the boys, like other versions, with the softness of her care; rather: "her elegant head pointed / toward something far beyond her," her body "narrow and finely-boned," "possessed, it seemed, of a great still / ness, like the saturated stillness of the roses, but tightly-nerved, / set, on the instant, to move."[165]

Three wolves in three distinct head positions: nurturing mother turned towards the boys, protector or inquisitor turned towards the viewer, and careful visionary looking far into whatever constitutes a wolfly distance. I think the sculptor would have been very glad to have Kelly see the difference. What might Luperca have been watching, or watching for? Perhaps her nose sensed some troubling scent in the air and she was discerning what it belonged to, or perhaps she sensed another kind of trouble stirring, the trouble of a snake that slithers between the feet of squabbling gods and kings. She knew something of our troubles and something of her own, and knew how to wind her body, "tightly-nerved," to fight them off. Or maybe it wasn't a question of past or present,

---

165. Brigit Pegeen Kelly, "Rome," *Ploughshares*, Vol. 35, No. 1 (Spring 2009), 104.

but of possible futures. Maybe she saw the possibilities of the place where she found the boys, one of them Rome, and had fed them while contemplating which future she would invoke. The boys could be a meal, after all. Or maybe she was consulting the mind of Mother Earth, whose thoughts she trusted as her own, listening in "saturated stillness" to the place and what it wanted to become. Perhaps she simply helped them because life helping life was the living thing to do. As Kelly's student, Darcie Dennigan, wrote eloquently in a reminiscence:

> What is asked *of* me not *by* me—must I honor that above all that I myself want? And I thought, Yes. Yes: if there is littleness. If it is a child or a creature or something large that is wounded. If it is a person without what they need, yes.[166]

To act as holy usher or hungry creature, to save the heart of the boy that would one day become the heart of Rome, or assimilate his heart into hers? Was their need greater than any of the others present in the encounter? I think all these possibilities, and more, were swirling. In any case, Luperca chose the self of emergency mother, chose the boys, chose Rome, gave them of her milk and heart, and her choice continues to influence even these final pages. Indeed, how far into the future "the she-wolf's litter" would extend—until now, until who knows when.

But it isn't merely a rosy story. Rome was founded in motherly milk and Rome was founded in fratricide and blood. Luperca stands over the boys in both care and protection from

---

166. Darcie Dennigan, https://kenyonreview.org/kr-online-is-sue/2020-septoct/selections/darcie-dennigan-656342/, accessed December 28, 2024.

murderous forces. Including the one inside her. Even the roses in this final poem, the roses Kelly so loved, were beautiful, yes, but also daggered with thorns. The connotation we give to rosy is wrong or incomplete. A false, imbalanced attention, the attention of one eye lit, the other eye shut against the dark. Here again is one of Kelly's key insistences: that we honor the full circumstances of biology's predicament: wonder and danger, blessing and horror, help and harm, gratitude and neglect, living and dying, suffering and transformation. Not one or the other. More than two sides of a coin. More than inextricably linked. Often both in the same instance, as the same being. Did the land want to become Rome, so Luperca helped it, or did Luperca ignore the land's pleas to kill the boys and their murderous souls, her heart moved by something other?

It's not *or*, it's *and*, or it's *or* and *and*. It seems like a contradiction, but contradictions are also complements from a more holistic perspective. In some versions of the story, a woodpecker assists Luperca in feeding the boys, land and sky collaborating in their survival.[167] Which is it? Both. The realms converge and the realms carry their own frequencies. We inhabit many, more than we can ever know. In this one, the one of this book and the one of this reader, the dark song sings a story of stories, plural. It isn't fixed, it isn't recordable. The song sings itself uniquely in each moment in each person. What a gift to hear the

167. Britannica.com, https://www.britannica.com/biography/Romulus-and-Remus, accessed December 30, 2024.

ones we do. To know that whatever forces conspired and guided Mars the rapist and Rhea the calculating mother, guided the servant against the king and Tibernius in the boys' deliverance, guided Luperca to give them life and Romulus to take it from his brother—clearly the forces assisted the boys in retaining their tenuous hold on life, shepherding the fragile spark of Rome and enabling it to grow a tough, survivor's long-lived heart. A heart that loves—not coddles—like a mother: nurturer, protector: *both*.

I think there's something of Kelly in the wolf looking out into the distance and choosing to instill in us the uncertainty of whatever the wolf considers. The stance of providence's protector, apprehensive against harm, while knowing death and undoing is providence's means of continuing to provide. To be alive: fragile and resilient, to come from death and die again: sweet release, bitter loss. To hold it all and feel like none of it can be held except as it flows through and away from us. The miraculous curse. And in rare instances, the chance to feel some small muscle-twitch of the future in one's fibers, then actively participate in its manifestation.

Kelly's contribution is shaping me now—the way she sees teaches me to see—and in all likelihood, will continue to shape me to my end. I want to return to the rest of the poem and the uniqueness of *her* vision. In Kelly's statue, the boys are "not babes, as one might expect, but two / lean boys."[168] They weren't yet given to human care, as they were in most accounts. They had stayed,

168. Brigit Pegeen Kelly, "Rome," *Ploughshares*, Vol. 35, No. 1 (Spring 2009), 104.

chosen to remain with Luperca, and she with them, had become "cut from the same shadowed stone." But there's something odd, something of the over-lingering addict in these boys, a rather unrosy possessiveness in their postures:

> [...] one boy
> pressing four fingers against one long breast, his other hand
> cupped beneath it to catch the falling milk, the second boy wrap-
> ping both arms around another breast, as if to carry it off, neither
> boy suckling, both instead turned toward you, dreamy, sweetly
> sly, as if to chide you for interrupting their feeding, or as if they
> were plotting a good trick...[169]

They're boys, not men, and their acts may be more childish misguidedness than mean, but clearly one appears to be forcing the milk from the teat rather than suckling, the other attaching himself to her like a tick, or a thief caught in the act. It's telling that the boys apprehend the viewer, rather than Luperca, boys a bit too old for this, boys of slyness, chiding and trickery. This is Kelly's vision, and the artist's: one of the ways the story goes. Perhaps it's less nefarious than it seems: necessary to the future, the extended fortification by his wolf-mother what Romulus needed to create and endure his destiny. Perhaps it's a warning against over-attachment, the boys clinging, Luperca indulging, both headed for a painful break.

I'm less inclined towards the latter interpretation—it's one of them, but my gut says Luperca wouldn't abide such behavior. Could she? Yes. Maybe there's another side of the story where the boys needed her protection longer than most imagine. I believe the bond is sweet, the kind of sweetness of which the heart lives. And

169. Ibid.

dies. Even Kelly turns her eye towards beauty at that moment, then widens the aperture from there:

> [...] Beautiful, those boys among the
> roses. Beautiful, the black wolf. But it was the breasts that held the
> eye, a double row of four black breasts, eight smooth breasts, each
> narrowing to a strict point, piercing sharp, exactly the shape of
> the ivory tooth of the shark.[170]

Ah, I see something now I haven't seen before. We're moving past the boys, who frankly take up too much room in the story for my liking. We're moving past Rome and humanity's future and returning to the real power in the story. It's not the boys. They're a speck. Rome will be a bigger speck but still a speck. Two thousand years? A tick, a whisper in time, forty-eight millionths of a percent, compared to the age of Mother Earth. The boys may be a portal to a species and its fantastic drama, but Luperca is a portal to the dark, to life itself and the life-creating, life-transcending forces that shape her understanding and acts.

In the final image, which the sculptor emphasized in stone, and Kelly chose to re-emphasize in words, we move past even Luperca to her breasts, both "smooth" and "narrowing to a strict point," the founts of life's milk, which are soft, yes, but also "piercing sharp, exactly the shape of / the ivory tooth of the shark." They give and they bite. Or what they give bites along the way. Each moment's a gift, the reception of which is a glory, yes, but also a sanding that wears us down. Shall we love life for both the beatings and the blessings? If we need to. If we're capable. To be

---

170. Ibid.

grateful for one and not the other doesn't invalidate gratitude. But turning a blind eye toward the dark may endanger our ability to endure. Kelly gives us the fullest vision she can: milk, bite, and the penetrating attentiveness that yields both gratitude and protection. As compelled as we are to be grateful, we're also compelled to care: care by nurture, and care by whatever it takes to protect. Again: to be grateful, but careful: a wise ethic, worth repeating.

Luperca carries that power within her, and that power—a divine yet Earthly, planetary power—carries Luperca within herself. Mother Earth carries the boys, Rome, us, wolves, deer, Kelly, gardens, cemeteries and lilies, is the artist in whose creation we are made and endowed with her ability to create, as she was endowed with her mother's. Life didn't and doesn't happen of its own accord. Nor did planets, nor stars. It's all wound in. Providence and participation. Creative, destructive, transformative, existential. A complexity unfathomable, fathoming in its entirety being but a brief melody in the score. *But this is the time of our melody*, so let us fathom while we can, while we are able to contemplate and attend, to embody a music so heart-breakingly beautiful it's heart-reviving, heart-making. Made more so when we feel ourselves immersed in the dark river of song, the song flowing in the air and in our blood, and choose to contribute, to receive the gift of voice and give in return: by adding our voices to the chorus.

Kelly's addition is a blessing, a gift, a nourishment: one I can never thank enough.

I turn at last, again, to the wisdom of Eleanor Wilner, who, in her introduction to the journal in which was "Rome" was published, adds her own voice to the chorus, deepening my sense of Kelly's contributions, penning sentences that feel made for me, and made for this story:

> I love poets who bring us to our proper size. Think about taking a picture of a mile-high waterfall, and about that little human figure you need in the shot to suggest the magnitude caught in the image—the tiny person is the scale factor. It isn't that true scale diminishes the human, but rather that it celebrates our luck to be in the picture at all—such wonders! I think of that simile from Anglo-Saxon poetry—of our lives as the flight of a sparrow across the lighted mead hall, from darkness to darkness, and bow to the poet whose image that was.[171]

That image was some antique poet's. And it was Mother Earth's—a poet of species. It was Grandmother Universe's—a poet of stars and galaxies. And that spirit of placing us in proper scale beside our kindred creatures, within the body of Mother Earth and all her intersecting realms, is Kelly's. And it is Wilner's (read her!). And it is ours, for now, while we and the sparrow can flap our wings and share this ancient flight.

Five poems. Were there more? I don't know, and I'm not going to ask. I looked hard—they're the traces I found. And Kelly's life is the last poem, a poem she inherited and a poem that continues beyond her. I purposely wrote this gushing admiration of a book without consulting anyone who knew Kelly personally, anyone who might erase part of the understanding and life I formed under the gift and influence of her books. A slightly dangerous

171. Eleanor Wilner, "Introduction," *Ploughshares*, Vol. 35, No. 1 (Spring 2009), 7.

mode of composition, to be sure, for what if I'm wrong? What if I'm deeply off base? What if many of my intimations, meditations and speculations neither square with their experience of Kelly, nor fit the facts as they're known? A deer whispers in my ear: "that's okay." And I believe the whisper, wherever it came from. To be wrong in one version of reality isn't to be wrong in them all. A wrongness may pervade many realms, or one, according to its kind and degree. According to what's going on. The laws we know become not laws but limitations of awareness in the light of older, larger laws. Laws that defy the limitations we believed in, laws that teach us the path isn't merely wrongfooted *or* rightfooted. It's a path of right-and-wrong in the left foot, wrong-and-right in the right, and vice versa, and both and neither, all at the same timeless time. A path of *is*, which includes the path of *isn't*. A path I both took and found myself taking to my great fortune.

To have proceeded as I did, not knowing—to have moved by intuition and felt my way through the mysteries of Kelly's realms—may have veiled me to biographical fact and the inside scoop, but it revealed to me another kind of understanding, the understanding of intimacy between reader and poetry, between lifeform and creation, Kelly's poems needing no intermediary to shape me. To teach me what they understand about life and how to live. To teach me that creatures and phenomena are not reducible or isolable facts, but active thrivings, each sensation an instant's glimpse into a near-infinite gravity of states and selves. Each state and self: worth living. Each state and self: worthy of attention. I came to know a few of Kelly's states. I came to share in a few of her selves, to invite her work into a few of mine, and to forge a few new ones through the alchemy of these mergers.

There are countless more in the work. Countless more realms to discover and books to be written. States and selves to realize. Minds to make and merge in the hydra of poetic spirit. I hope this book is a start, a drop of affection that lends the warmth of its candleflame to kindred admirers of Kelly's work and nudges them to write their own. If there's a wealth of affection out there, as I know there is, why not write more books? I hope I live to see them. I hope they continue to emerge long after I'm gone. These books, your books. They would each be a gift. A hoof-print, a wing-flap, a lily-god, a wolf-mother, a deer's head emerging in the mist, a stone hand tilting a cup for five hundred years, watering a thirsty heart. These books would be the embodiment of a shared soul, a continuance of Kelly, who so greatly deserves the loving carriage. For my part, it would enable me to love her work that much more. I'd be so grateful for your help as you introduce me to the realms I couldn't find.

I close my eyes and cast my sense of feeling out towards those realms now, and I sense a flicker of movement, just past the orchards and gardens, past the cemeteries of our beloved ancestors, somewhere at the edge of a forest, where dusk fades to darkness. It's the movement of creatures and energies, feeding and being fed—the familiarity born of that communion, finding sources of nourishment and sharing them, watching one another's backs. I sense the movement, and then, I'm there, animal, a mysterious shapeshifting amidst the herd of our books, a wolf-and-deer-pack that would, finally, become a collaboration of gratitude and care. And nowhere in this vast, many-minded spirit can I think of a better homage than that.

Afterword

I hope it's clear by now that I wrote this book out of admiration and adoration. I love Kelly's work. For what it is, as much as for the influence it has on me, on the way I see and feel and live, on the way I comprehend and participate in art. On what and how I write. Influence is a wonderful, complex, tricky thing. A blessing. And a risk. The word's etymological shadow contains various states and traits: to flow in; an emanation from the stars affecting one's fate; the power to teach, shape, guide, even possess, control and direct. Like most things, it can be taken too far. Think of what it means to be under the influence of drugs, alcohol— spirits. A little can enliven and enrich. More than a little can be used to reboot the mind, make breakthroughs, make nights to remember, make art that no one forgets. More than that can hasten the hourglass in your heart. Create blackout nights where you're no longer present to witness your demon's actions. My own father died of an overdose after forty years of addiction. Laced drugs, bad luck, an unfortunate end, but a danger which he had courted and learned to dance with like a Nijinsky of getting high. I hated his life choices as a teenager, but then I learned: it's what he needed to bear the pressures of this life, to find the joy and beauty in the hardships and suffering, those of poverty and those of simply being alive.

I danced with those devils myself, accidentally overdosing as a teenager, but whereas my father died, someone found me on the sidewalk and ferried me to the hospital, where the doctors pumped my stomach and told death to fuck off before it was too late. I'm telling you this because when I woke up, I didn't quit drugs. I turned to another one, the spiritual drug of art, specifically poetry. It kept me interested and gave me a lifelong practice in something I could never perfect, something that would always remain two steps ahead, saying *come forward, come forward.* It gave me something to do and care about, and any means of caring is a means of staying alive.

Make no mistake: poetry is a spirit, *an emanation from the stars affecting one's fate*, a possession that impacts one's way of seeing, feeling, believing, being and behaving. But it's a sprit whose possession of my life has kept me tethered, grateful, not sane in the traditional sense, but sane in the sense of trying to learn to live on the terms by which the world turns, not the terms I might try to impose on the world according to a certain species' theories. Learning to live by the world's terms is as impossible as artistic perfection is, but the endeavor keeps me going, interested in existing, if not always in love with how existence happens. Poetry is also defeating, lonely, exhausting and really effing hard. To work at this with skill and heart is truly a spiritual, some might even say monastic, undertaking. No one can do the work for you. No one can make the frustrations, failures and rejections easier to bear. But they can keep you company while you pick up the pieces of your heart.

Poems and poets can be amazing, nourishing company. Some poets can make it all worthwhile, even when you're not sure you have what it takes, when you think you're getting nowhere and want to call it quits. Some poets can unstuck you, remind you of the brief moments of magic, be the pair of tweezers you need to remove a spiritual thorn. Some poets can even be so magical, they become one of your reasons for continuing, a saving grace you can turn to when everything else loses its color and breath. Kelly is such a poet for me. A heart-reviving medicine, a reason to read, a reason to live, a reason to write. Returning to the spirit of her work, opening myself to possession by her particular influence—it invigorates and guides me.

She's also a model to hold my own efforts against to see if they measure up. And therein lies the danger. One method of training as a poet is to find the poets who deeply move (or infuriate) you, then try to emulate their work, to live inside their themes and rhythms and sentences, learning some of the secrets of their architecture, and hopefully imbibing enough of their nourishment to let it kindle your own magic. But there's a time to imbibe and a time to turn away. Some poets get stuck on the dope and continue to partake, imagining the intoxication will lead them to a state from which to produce a similar greatness, avoiding the hard, essential work, the sweat of transmutation. Other poets want to be as skilled and as well-known as their favorites, want it so badly, they try to adopt the measures of accomplishment their models used as their own. They hold their work against the work they love, and turn away defeated, time and again, wondering why they can't yield the same power, while the power they actually yield may be quite moving, just born from a register unique to themselves. Worse, some poets try to wear the skin of their idols, even when it doesn't fit, dreaming of being the vehicle of reincarnation, and when that doesn't work, undertaking the dark art of summoning a spirit that doesn't want to be summoned. It all ends poorly.

So we return to Kelly's counsel: to be grateful but careful, to drink from her visions and offerings when we need them, but then to turn, to journey, to see and feel and make, both for ourselves and for those who need us as sources of influence and nourishment in turn. There's the rub, for me: influence is inheritance, born of the stars which were born of the dark, born of the Earth and passed into life, born of Rilke and passed into Kelly, born of Kelly and passed into poets, like me, who find her poems and presences inspiring. Influence, for me, well received and well handled, is a gift we don't own but shepherd, a gift to be tended, added to, and passed along.

When I look back at my own octet of influences in light of the words above, I think I'm lucky: the poets I most love and most draw inspiration from are poets I couldn't mimic for the life of me. There's something about them, a deepening or enlargening of heart, soul, attentiveness, intelligence, understanding and care, a way of being and saying that quiets my senses and awakens me to a greater abundance and complexity in the world, sending me as often into the day and contemplation as into the next poem. They're spiritual drugs so potent it's best for me to take a couple hits and move along, overindulging either leading to them overtaking me or knocking me out. I speak from experience: I've read too much and been stunned, unable to write, unable to think. So I learned to respect the influence, the power of the medicine, and the responsibility to use it wisely, and to try to teach responsible usage in turn. And I've gone against my own advice: I've tried and tried to emulate my idols, too many times: it didn't work. It turns out that's a good thing. Maybe that's the sign of a good influence: one we can learn from, share in, and teach, but one that tends to turn us back towards the responsibility of our own work. The work of our own poems, and the work of the poets who trust us to help and guide them.

All told, Kelly has helped me immensely. I could say how for another fifty pages, but I already did that: the impacts of her influence are everywhere in this book. She helped me, and that's the most I could ask for. So I'd like to end by sharing a poem of my own, a poem that feels born under the star of Kelly, a beneficiary of her help. It's the only poem I ever wrote of its kind and it poured through me like a fever and it was frankly a blazing mess. I wasn't thinking about Kelly when I wrote it and I hadn't read her for close to a year, but a while after it was written, after I'd tried and failed to tame it, after teachers and friends had tried and failed to tame its form, I began to sense something of Kelly hovering in its *atmosphere.*

That's one of Kelly's gifts—she worked exquisitely in the common gold of images, but she also worked in a rarer gold of atmospheres, something felt but not seen, a quality of air, light, breath and inner weather that pushes depth and dimension into the scenes, pushes the poem into the reader and the reader into the poem. Kelly's friend Joy Manesiotis remarked on this aspect of her work, "I have that sense: that the poem builds in the reader and then the reader is taken aback to find a whole constructed thing inside them."[172] I think she's right, that poems, once imbibed, tend to live in our heads, a few descending into our hearts, our guts, or something we cannot name. And that Kelly's poems tend to take

172. Plumepoetry.com, https://plumepoetry.com/uncover-ing-what-is-brave-a-remembrance-of-brigit-pegeen-kelly-by-joy-ma-nesiotis-and-maxine-scates/, accessed December 31, 2024.

up residence in the blood and circulate throughout the body, hence the initial response of shock, of being stunned, a slow widening of the eyes.

I think that's an effect of her atmospheres, and that the embodiment moves outward as well as inward. Kelly's poems do both: they fully embody us, and they create fully embodied worlds that we suddenly inhabit, worlds neither safe nor familiar but instinctively an extension of the worlds we know, a peeling back of the story of *how we think life works*—the critical reduction of sensorial information without which every moment would overwhelm us—to reveal a layer of *how life lives, how life thinks on its own terms*, a thinking overheard in the instrument of Brigit, the whole of our tiny geographies of knowledge included in life's incomprehensible mind, a mind made a little more knowable via Kelly's sensitive hearing.

And it's this atmospheric quality that I felt in this poem I wrote—or was a conduit for, properly speaking—and that made me aware of Kelly's presence. Is that wishful thinking? Perhaps. But is wishful thinking also an attempt to catch a glimpse of a trace one cannot fully comprehend? I think so. I had Wendell Berry in mind more than I had Kelly in mind at the time, and I can sense some of his influence in the shadows, too, but I see more of Kelly's influence each time I look. The poem was wild and refused to be tamed. Finally I shoved all the lines together like one of Kelly's in *The Orchard* and it clicked, at least for me. And the poem is a wilderness that compelled me to enter its world, a world that felt neither safe nor familiar but necessary, a shadow animal I followed, not quite knowing why, but with an intuition that it had something to show me.

It did. It showed me another way that life works. And I may have been the instrument for that particular poetic spirit to find expression, but I couldn't have prepared myself to receive the expression if I hadn't had reams of help. I had the help of Kelly. And Berry. And Wilner. And Rilke. I had help from the spirit of poetry, giving me a reason to live, and to contribute, one word, one breath at a time. And I hope, for whoever needs to read this, that this book, and this poem, are a reason to keep breathing in turn.

If I can be of any help, please consider the portal to my inbox open.

SOMEWHERE IN INDIANA

About twenty klicks east of the Mississippi, rain fills a bucket with hope, but the bucket leaks, has been sitting so long with its rust whispering henna to dirt, the black dirt, that the farm it once belonged to has faded from memory, as have the forms of value that lead from seed to mouth, where generations of teeth crumble and fall out, and kids develop poorly not for lack of something to eat but for lack of nutrients in their food, and the land that used to be a farm that used to be a cougar's valley has changed hands many times, it has passed between people that never once dug their fingers into the Earth's body, never once felt her cool shiver as they brought her dark soul I mean soil into the light, never carried her with them indoors, never spent five minutes digging her out from under their nails, they've never known this pleasure, they call it labor and shudder at the thought, like a filthy deed, like a punishment to be avoided, oblivious to the dullness in their eyes and their speech, where the names for things have receded into words like bird and tree and flower, they titter with self-pleasure at the dullness it takes bad sex and liquor to shine, but the bucket lives by another code, the bucket has stood still in the weeds for decades, become an elder to the malnourished children who come and kick it like a cheap headstone, or a relic, or a cup for extinct ogres, and when it rains, the hole in the bucket, so packed with leaves it leaks slowly like the sun, the hole asks the Earth to breathe up through the water, to softly sing, and she does, and for those who have the ears to hear it, her song fills the whole valley, and at dusk the deer poke their heads from the woods, they follow the sound, stepping gingerly but surely, like hearts to hope, like children to promise, and if you saw it, the movement of their lips as they lowered their heads to drink, you might think they were whispering vespers to the bucket, or to the Earth as she sings to them, some low lullaby of praise in deersong like thank you, bucket, for being here, for taking a long time to depart, we count on you to wet our lips when the clouds fail to appear, they don't fill the sky like they used to, the sky bleeds with the barks of dogs and the shouts of men who loose their dogs upon us for fun, men who wouldn't even know what to do with our bodies if we died, let alone know how to bury us so we won't haunt them, and we will, we will fill them with a dread so subtle it feels like their own failure, but enough of them, we love you, bucket, and we think of you as we lose the dogs in the brush, as we approach you from across the valley, everything coated in thin white dust, and when we settle into our dens at night, we talk of you, as one might talk of a cupped hand, fading slowly, the rest of the body long departed: a rusty bucket, offering water—all that's left of a god.

ACKNOWLEDGEMENTS

My deep and abiding gratitude, as always, to Aaron Kent, for his kind and generous support of me and my work in so many of its incarnations. There are all kinds of publishers. To have one, like Aaron, who not only appreciates my weirdness, but is always understanding when I'm a messy, reclusive, delinquent human being, is an invaluable medicine. Truly, he and the whole Broken Sleep family are a blessing, and to work with them is, among other things, a healing of old wounds.

My endless gratitude to Jenny Boully, Carmen Smith and Craig Morgan Teicher, too, who helped me tap a latent capacity for criticism, and offered gentle but deeply meaningful nudges as they let me find my own way into the practice. And to Melissa Febos, whose work showed me how personal and passionate literary contemplation could be, and gave me hope that there might be a way I could do this *and love doing it.*

And to Mama Gaia, our eco-spirit, who gives me breath, mind, soul and the ability to write this: I pray this is a good use of these gifts. And to Brigit, of course, for everything: your work and spirit counsel me in writing, thinking, perceiving, being and believing, and so often, when I find myself caught in stuckedness or wallowing in failure, I sip from the nourishment of your gifts, and find myself encouraged to keep trying. And to my wife, Safora, and my soul dog, Addie, whose companionship and heart keep me tethered, loved and warm: my favorite poems are the poems we live together.

LAY OUT YOUR UNREST

www.ingramcontent.com/pod-product-compliance
Lightning Source LLC
Chambersburg PA
CBHW032228080426
42735CB00008B/762